# SOUTHERN PACIFIC

# SOUTHERN PACIFIC

## Bill Yenne

**Bonanza**
NEW YORK

Published 1988 by
Bonanza Books, distributed by
Crown Publishers Inc.

Produced by Brompton Books Corp.
15 Sherwood Place
Greenwich, CT 06830, USA

Printed in Hong Kong

Library of Congress Cataloging in Publication data:

1. Southern Pacific Railroad – History 2. Railroads – United States – History. 1. Title.
HE2791.S794Y46   1985   388   85-5698
ISBN 0-516-46084X

ISBN 0-517-46084X

h g f e d c

## Acknowledgments

The author would like to thank Bob Sederholm and Andy Anderson at Southern Pacific for their kind assistance both with background information and for supplying photographs from the Southern Pacific archives. Thanks are also due Rod Baird, Kathy Jaeger, Vic Reyna and George Young for their help and support through the project; and to Carol Yenne for typing the manuscript.

Design and cartography by Bill Yenne

Edited by Susan Garratt

*Page 1:* **Workers assemble for a 1924 photograph outside the Sacramento Shops, where Southern Pacific locomotives, including** *No 3685,* **were built.**

*Page 2/3: No 4449* **in** *Daylight* **livery belches out a full head of steam as it rounds a bend in the Siskiyous. Southern Pacific donated** *No 4449* **to the city of Portland, Oregon, in 1958.**

*Below: No 5009* **was one of the last of Southern Pacific's 4-10-2 oil-burning locomotives.**

## Picture Credits

All photographs were provided by the **Southern Pacific Company,** with the following exceptions:

**The Bancroft Library, University of California, Berkeley** 26, 28-9, 41, 72 (bottom), 92
**Jon Brenneis, Southern Pacific** 111 (right)
**Tom Brown, Southern Pacific** 110 (top right), 113, 117 (top)
**Charles Fox, Southern Pacific** 107 (bottom), 110 (bottom), 125 (bottom)
**Thomas Lea, Southern Pacific** 111 (left)
**National Railway Historical Society** 21 (bottom), 24, 24-25
**Vic F Reyna** 95 (both)
**Santa Fe Railway** 118
**Bob Sederholm, Southern Pacific** 125 (top)
**Southern Pacific via Association of American Railroads** 13, 20-21, 31, 40
**Southern Pacific via National Railway Historical Society** 55
**Union Pacific via Association of American Railroads** 22-23
© **Bill Yenne** 10 (both), 11 (both), 82, 83, 86, 112, 124 (both), 126-27

# Contents

# A Golden Dream
## 1850-1861

The story of American industrial expansion in the nineteenth century is the story of the visionary men who guided the nation during its growth years. It was these men who created the framework upon which men of lesser ambition were able to build their lives, their fortunes and their own smaller empires. It was the great industrial giants of America's period of expansion who built the nation's infrastructure, her cities, her factories, her railroads. Without the railroads the Industrial Revolution would never have spread across Europe, and without the railroads the United States would never have sprawled across the North American continent.

The story of Southern Pacific is the story of five men whose foresight helped turn the dream of a steel track connecting the halves of a continent into an actuality. Four of these men turned the myth of California into a reality. It was the empire they created that bound together not only California, but the whole region that became known a century later as the Sun Belt.

Gold was discovered at Sutter's Mill in the western slopes of the Sierra Nevada in January 1848, and thousands of people flocked to California in the ensuing gold rush. California became a state of the Union in 1850, and in 1854 Sacramento was made its capital. Included in the hordes who swept across the wilderness and around Cape Horn were dozens who came to build vast fortunes in the new land and succeeded. Among them were the five men upon whose dreams the Southern Pacific was built: Collis P Huntington, Leland Stanford, Charles Crocker, Mark Hopkins and Theodore Judah.

### Judah Comes to California

Theodore Dehone Judah, a civil engineer from the environs of Troy, New York, arrived in Sacramento in 1854 at the behest of the Sacramento Valley Rail Road Company (SVRR). With the Sacramento business community behind it, the SVRR had been incorporated in 1852 with plans for a railroad to connect that city with the gold fields of the Sierra, and Judah was the man picked to engineer the line. He was prepared to do the job, but his vision was fixed on a larger idea: a transcontinental line that would connect California to the rest of the nation. Judah was by no means the only one dreaming that dream. Pioneer railroad promoter Asa Whitney had first proposed the idea seriously in 1845, and after statehood was achieved, there were many who clamored for better access to the East.

California was in a curious position. It was a state of the Union but it was not contiguous with any other territory that was also a state, and for all the difficulty of communication it

**Theodore Judah (right), first came west to engineer the SVRR, whose locomotive Sacramento (below) was California's first.**

may as well have been a different continent. Transporting cargo between San Francisco and the East by sea meant a trip of several months around the tip of South America. Transporting goods overland required a difficult journey through the jungles of the Isthmus of Panama. The trip across the continent itself was also a grueling experience of several months' duration that involved encounters with a variety of natural obstacles and unpredictable Indians. Two ranges of high mountains, the Rockies and the Sierra Nevada, made crossing the continent with any significant wagon load perilous at best and impossible in winter. Four years before California became a state, 87 members of a group of pioneers en route west from Illinois, known as the Donner party, had either frozen or starved to death in the Sierra just a hundred miles short of Sacramento.

It was against this backdrop that Theodore Judah went to work on the Sacramento Valley Rail Road, which was completed in 1856. On 22 February of that year, the locomotive *Sacramento*, a 4-4-0 carried around Cape Horn by ship, left the state capital with cars that carried the first paying customers to travel by train in California. It was less than five years since a locomotive of Missouri's Pacific Railroad had made the first run west of the Mississippi River, but still there was half a continent between them.

His first western railroad complete, Judah became one of the leading exponents of a transcontinental, or 'Pacific,' railroad as it was known then. When Asa Whitney first suggested such a railroad in 1845, his was a decidedly minority voice. However, by the time Theodore Judah arrived in Washington, DC, in late 1856 to lobby Congress for funding, the idea had grown in popularity. Senator Thomas Hart Benton of Missouri had placed the idea before Congress in 1849, and Pacific railroad conventions had been held in Memphis, New Orleans and Boston that same year. It seemed as though the gold rush had won many converts to the dream of a railroad to the West.

The only question, apparently, was that of what route the new road would take. The central route to the Pacific followed the major overland routes of the day and was the shortest distance between San Francisco and chief western embarkation points like St Louis and Kansas City. Advocates of a northern route pointed out that the nature of the navigable Mississippi/Missouri River network made Puget Sound 700 miles closer than San Francisco. The southern route, too, had many advocates. In 1853 Secretary of War (and later President of the Confederacy) Jefferson Davis of Mississippi presented a 13-volume study of nine possible southern routes, which, it was pointed out, were largely free of snow and high mountain passes. The Gadsden Purchase of 1854 made these routes all the more attractive.

Judah was a delegate to the 1859 Pacific Railroad Convention in Washington, DC, and he presented the case for the central route. Though Congress was still not ready to subsidize the idea, Judah was not discouraged. Back in California the following year, he began to survey possible routes through the Sierra. At the urging of Dr Daniel Strong of Dutch Flat, Judah considered a possible course between that town and Truckee, north of Lake Tahoe. The Dutch Flat route was exactly what Judah had hoped for, and he publicly announced his findings – an indiscretion that cost him his job with the SVRR. Undeterred, he set off in November 1860 for

San Francisco, the gleaming metropolis that the gold rush had turned into a major financial center in less than a decade. His objective was to find the financial backing necessary to build the railroad of his dreams, but one after another, the Market Street financiers turned him down. Judah returned to Sacramento, where he found a more auspicious reception for his ideas.

## The Big Four

In Sacramento, Theodore Judah was introduced to four merchants who had come west in the wake of the gold rush to set up shop in California's capital. While Judah had been building the SVRR and pursuing his dream in the East, Charles Crocker had been presiding over a dry goods establishment and Mark Hopkins and Collis Huntington over a hardware store; grocer Leland Stanford had been a rising star in the state's new Republican Party. Meeting with Judah above the Huntington-Hopkins store, the four merchants gradually developed an enthusiasm for Judah's idea and for the prospect of turning Sacramento into a major commercial hub. They were also interested in sharing the mineral wealth that lay on the eastern side of the Sierra, where a major discovery of silver had just been made near Virginia City, Nevada.

On 28 June 1861 they formed the Central Pacific Railroad, forerunner of the empire that was called the Southern Pacific. The Central Pacific was incorporated under the laws of California and dedicated to building a railroad across the Sierra via Dutch Flat. Leland Stanford became president of the new firm and Collis Huntington became its vice-president. The frugal Mark Hopkins was named treasurer and James Bailey,

the jeweler who had introduced Judah to the Big Four, was made secretary. Judah became chief engineer and Crocker formed Charles Crocker and Company, a wholly owned subsidiary that was to undertake construction of the Central Pacific.

The offices of the Central Pacific were located at 56 and 58 K Street, between Second and Third streets and adjoining the Huntington-Hopkins Hardware store at 54 K Street.

Leland Stanford was born on 9 March 1824, the son of a Watervliet, New York, tavern owner, and he attended the Clinton Liberal Institute and Casenovia Seminary before going west to practice law in Port Washington, Wisconsin. When gold was discovered in California, two of his brothers

## The Golden Dream

**1850-52** The Big Four (Charles Crocker, Mark Hopkins, Collis Huntington and Leland Stanford) arrive in Sacramento.

**1854** Theodore Judah arrives in Sacramento to engineer the Sacramento Valley Rail Road.

**1856** The Sacramento Valley Rail Road, the first railroad in California, is completed.

**1860** Judah announces the discovery of a suitable trans-Sierra railroad route.

**1861** The Central Pacific Railroad is incorporated on 28 June with Leland Stanford as president, Collis Huntington as vice-president, Mark Hopkins as treasurer and Theodore Judah as chief engineer. Charles Crocker forms the construction company that will build the railroad. Leland Stanford is elected governor of California.

*Above, from left:* **The legendary Big Four joined forces to build the Central Pacific across the Sierra Nevada: Collis P Huntington served as vice-president; Leland Stanford as president; Charles Crocker as president of Charles Crocker and Company and as construction supervisor; and Mark Hopkins as treasurer.**

joined the gold rush, and when his law practice was gutted by fire in 1852, Leland Stanford followed them west. He settled in Sacramento, where he opened a store selling groceries and supplies to miners. He amassed an early fortune when he took mine shares as payment for a store debt and the mine turned out to be a rich one. Stanford turned to politics and was nominated by the Republican Party as its candidate for governor on 21 June 1861, nine days before the Central Pacific was incorporated. The Civil War had just broken out, and Stanford ran on a platform of keeping California in the Union, a goal which would certainly be served by a transcontinental railroad that assumed the central route. Stanford was elected California's first Republican governor in November 1861, and although he served in the post for only a single two-year term, he continued to be known almost universally as 'Governor Stanford,' even after he was elected to the US Senate in 1885.

Collis P Huntington, first vice-president of the new Central Pacific, was the financial mastermind among the Big Four. He was born in Harwinton, Connecticut, on 22 October 1821 and at the age of 14 he borrowed money to begin a clock-selling business. He parlayed his profits from this venture into a share in an Oneonta, New York, general store in partnership with his brother Solon. In 1850 he followed the gold rush to California, where he opened the hardware store with Mark Hopkins, another emigrant from the East. Gifted in his role as financier for the group, Huntington went to New York in December 1862, a month before construction of the Central Pacific began. From the New York offices, he managed brilliantly the fiscal development of the Central Pacific.

Born in Henderson, New York, in 1813, Mark Hopkins was

the oldest and most ascetic in both manner and appearance of the Big Four. Quiet of mood and lean of frame, 'Uncle' Mark Hopkins was noted for his thriftiness. It was said that he knew how to squeeze 106 cents of value out of every dollar.

Charles Crocker was born in Troy, New York, on 16 September 1822, but he moved to Indiana with his parents at the age of 14. In 1850 he crossed the plains to join the gold rush and was the only one of the Big Four to actually work as a miner. By 1856, however, he was a Sacramento merchant like the others, and, like them, a member of the Republican Party. As president of Charles Crocker and Company, formed by the Big Four to build the Central Pacific, he supervised the work himself. With Hopkins and Stanford ensconced in Sacramento and Huntington in New York, it was not at all unusual to see Charlie Crocker slogging through the mud and snow of the high Sierra as the tracks were laid.

Personal relations among the Big Four (they preferred to be called 'the Associates') were not always on the best of terms, and were frequently on the worst of terms. These men were nevertheless uniquely and ideally suited for the partnership in which they found themselves. Each contributed something to a whole that was greater than the sum of its parts, and that whole was transformed into the greatest commercial empire that had yet been seen on the western side of the continent.

# The Golden Spike
## 1862-1869

On 1 October 1861, having spent his summer in the Sierra, Theodore Judah reported to the directors of the Central Pacific that a practical route had been found. On 6 January 1862, Leland Stanford was inducted into office as governor of California, and he found himself in a unique position to put resources behind the building of the Central Pacific. In his inaugural address, Stanford told a Sacramento crowd that 'Within a short time the territory of Nevada has sprung into great importance [with a silver strike]; her vast undeveloped wealth will attract and give employment to an immense population of industrious and thriving people, ensuring her a brilliant and important destiny. From California she will necessarily derive most of her supplies. The most difficult link of the Pacific railroad which must pass through this Territory lies in California. It is not necessary at this late date to go into a general argument to prove the importance of a railroad connecting the Pacific and Atlantic Oceans, especially now, when its military necessity is so much more than ever apparent. I allude to it briefly because I think the time has arrived when, in consequence of local business, the most difficult and important part of the work can be accomplished without direct pecuniary aid from the national government. May we not therefore, with the utmost propriety even at this time, ask the National Government to donate lands and loan its credit in aid of this portion of that communication [the Pacific railroad] which is of the very first importance, not alone to the states and territories west of the Rocky Mountains, but to the whole nation, and is the great work of the age.'

Across the continent another Republican, President Abraham Lincoln, shared the vision. Presiding over a nation embroiled in a struggle for its survival, Lincoln could see that keeping California and the wealth of California and Nevada in the Union was essential. With the Union at war with the South, the southern transcontinental route was clearly not available, so the central route long favored by Judah was selected. Lincoln signed the Pacific Railroad Act on 1 July 1862, creating the Union Pacific Railroad Company to build a line westward from Omaha, Nebraska. The act authorized the Central Pacific to 'Start at or near San Francisco or some point on the navigable waters of the Sacramento River and build eastwardly to the western boundary of California, and

*Above:* **Leland Stanford, Central Pacific President and California Governor, wielded a silver spade on 8 January 1863 and set the dream of a transcontinental railroad in motion.**

*Right:* **Construction gangs at work in the Sierra, helped make the dream of the transcontinental come true.**

*Next page:* **The *C P Huntington*, Central Pacific's third locomotive, was later renumbered as Southern Pacific Number 1 and is now preserved in the California State Railroad Museum.**

. . . continue construction until meeting the line of the Union Pacific.'

It also provided for generous land grants to both railroads, allowed advance payments and eased security for loans. The Central Pacific received a land grant of 10 sections per mile, and the credit available from the use of government bonds to

*Above: C P Huntington* began service in 1864. This photograph was taken during construction over the Sierra.

*Left:* The 1868 financial statement for the Central Pacific Railroad, its seventh year of operation.

the amount of $16,000 per mile to the western base of the Sierra (as picked by California State Geologist J D Whitney), $48,000 for 150 miles over the mountains and $32,000 per mile across Nevada. The bonds constituted a first mortgage on the Central Pacific, with principal and interest payable in 30 years. (The government supplied bond credit rather than cash because it had used its cash to finance the war effort.) The Central Pacific accepted the terms of the act on 1 November 1862, but no investors could be found to undertake the building of the Union Pacific until the terms were liberally amended in 1864. There has long been some controversy concerning the designation of the western base of the Sierra and hence the point at which the Central Pacific began receiving government bond credit of $48,000 per mile as opposed to $16,000 per mile. Professor Whitney explained his decision:

'The point where the line of the Central Pacific Railroad crossed Arcade Creek may with propriety be taken as the base of the Sierra, as from there it commences a regular and continuous ascent, and in a distance of 150 miles from that point, the most difficult and mountainous portion of the route will have been traversed.' This placed the base of the Sierra seven miles from Sacramento, rather than at Newcastle, 31 miles away, as some critics insisted.

**Locomotive *No 1, Governor Stanford,* amid piles of steel rails in the Sacramento Yard c1864 during construction of the Sierra route.**

In any event, the Central Pacific needed to build 40 miles of track before any federal money would become available, so the Big Four set about selling shares in their company to raise the capital needed to begin. The financiers of San Francisco were still as dubious as they had been two years before, when Judah had gone to seek investment. Commercial paper was earning 12 percent for investors, and this notion of a railroad across the Sierra was a foolhardy investment by comparison. Shipping interests also were opposed to the railroad, which, if successful, would eat into their profits. The Sitka Ice Company, which imported the ice with which San Franciscans chilled their steam beer, was afraid of possible competition from Sierra ice that could be delivered more easily to San Francisco by rail. In the face of this initial adversity, the railroad was financed by the Big Four themselves.

**Across the Sierra**

On 8 January 1863, Governor Leland Stanford, wielding a silver spade, broke ground at Front and K streets in Sacramento and the dream was on its way to becoming a reality. After Theodore Judah completed his surveys and as the railroad was gradually built westward, his role began to diminish. Though he still referred to it as 'my little road,' it clearly belonged to the four 'associates' who were financing and building it. Animosity developed between Judah and Huntington, so Judah decided to go east to seek the financing

necessary to buy out his partners. He arranged a series of meetings in New York and left San Francisco by steamer in October 1863. When he crossed through the jungles of Panama, he contracted yellow fever, and on 2 November he died in New York at the age of 38.

Judah had died an exile from the enterprise that was his fondest dream, but the dream lived on. As governor during the first year of Central Pacific construction, Stanford was able to aid the railroad with land grants and by approving a $500,000 state subsidy that passed 28 to 4 in the state legislature. The subsidy was popularly supported at the time, despite the appearance of conflict of interest when considered a century and a quarter later. An editorial in the *Sacramento Union* commented that 'The act shows the world that the State feels bound to advance some of her means, and lend the weight of all her moral and political influence, to promote this national enterprise.' The subsidy was never paid, and was superseded by an arrangement for the state to pay 7 percent interest on $1,500,000 of company bonds.

On 7 October 1863, the Central Pacific's first locomotive arrived in Sacramento; on 9 November, having been dubbed *Governor Stanford,* it made its first run. On 25 April 1864, the first Central Pacific passenger service to Roseville began, and by 3 June the line had been extended to Newcastle. As the line reached into the mountains, the going became more difficult. It was made worse when the city of San Francisco held up the issuance of $400,000 in bonds approved by its voters in May 1863 (it was April 1865 before they were released), and by a labor shortage created by desertions from the railroad camps to the more lucrative mines.

Charles Crocker, who had been impressed with the industriousness of Chinese workers and eager to address the labor shortage, urged his foreman, J H Strobridge, to hire a crew of Chinese workers. As Crocker later recalled, 'I had a great deal of trouble to get Mr Strobridge to try Chinamen (*sic*). At first I recollect that four or five of the Irishmen on pay day got to talking together and I said to Mr Strobridge there is some trouble ahead. When I saw this trouble was impending, a committee came to ask for an increase of wages. I told Mr Strobridge then to go over to Auburn [near Sacramento] and get some Chinamen and put them to work. The result was the Irishmen begged us not to have any Chinamen come, and they resumed their work. It was four or five months after that before I could get Mr Strobridge to take Chinamen. Finally he took in fifty Chinamen, and a while after, he took fifty more. Then they did so well that . . . he got more and more until finally we got all we could use, until at one time I think we had ten or twelve thousand.'

In later years it was widely circulated that the Chinese workers were paid at a lower rate than white workers. In fact, company records show that everyone was paid at the same rate, a dollar a day. The discrepancy probably arises from the fact that white workers ate meals provided free by the company. The Chinese refused the company meals, which consisted of generous portions of bacon and beans, and they

opted for setting up their own kitchens. Ironically, the Chinese diet of vegetables, fruit and fish was a good deal healthier than bacon and beans. Later, on the Nevada desert when bad water was a problem, the Chinese avoided dysentery by boiling their water for tea.

On 30 November 1866, the line reached Cisco, about five hours by rail from Sacramento. It remained there for a year while the back-breaking work of punching the tunnels through the Sierra summit was undertaken. Drills and black-powder blasting were used for most of the job, which was painfully slow. Nitroglycerine was brought in for the main 1659-foot summit tunnel, and between February and April 1867 over 2000 blasts were made in the unrelenting granite.

Construction of the Union Pacific had finally gotten under way on 5 November 1865, nearly three years behind the Central Pacific, but the work was moving considerably faster. Laying tracks across the wonderfully flat expanses of Nebraska prairie bore no similarity to the difficulties en-countered in the Sierra. While the Central Pacific had its sights set on completing its line east across Nevada and part of Utah to Salt Lake, Union Pacific surveyors had laid out a route westward all the way to the California border.

The Sierra summit tunnels, begun even before the tracks reached Cisco, took two painful years to complete. These years, 1866 to 1868, included the two worst winters on

**PACIFIC RAILROAD.**

Time Table No. 6.    To take effect Feb. 14, 1865.

| TRAINS GOING EAST. | | Distance fr. Sac. | STATIONS. | Dist fr. N. | TRAINS GOING WEST | |
|---|---|---|---|---|---|---|
| Freight. No. 3. | Mail & Pass., No. 1. | | | | Mail & Pass, No. 2. | Freight, No. 4 |
| 2 P.M.. Dp.......... | 6.30 A.M. Dp.......... | | Sacramento.. | 31.. | 11.50 A.M Arr.... | 7.25 P M. Arr........ |
| 2.35 .................. | 6.55 ................ .. | 7 .. | Arcade........ | 24 . | 11.25 .............. | 6.55 .......... .... |
| 3.00 .................. | 7.10 .................. | 15.. | Antelope ..... | 16.. | 11.10 .............. | 6.30 .......... ...... |
| 3.25 ........ ..... | 7.20.................. | 18.. | Junction ..... | 13.. | 11 00 .............. | 6.15 .......... ........ |
| 3.45 .................. | 7.30.................. | 22.. | Rocklin ...... | 9... | 10.45 .............. | 5.50 .......... ........ |
| 4.05.................. | 7.40............ ...... | 25.. | Pino .......... | 6... | 10.35 .......... ... | 5 32.......... ........ |
| 4.40 P. M. Arr.....| 8.00 A M Arr........ | 31.. | Newcastle ... | | 10.15 A.M. Dp... | 5.00 P.M. Dp ........ |

No Trains will leave any Station ahead of time, unless specially ordered by Superintendent.
Gravel and Extra Trains must keep ten minutes out of the way of all regular Trains.
NIGHT SIGNALS.—A light swung over the head is a signal to go ahead.
When swung across, or at right angles with the track, is a signal to back up, and when moved up and down, is a signal to stop.

**C. CROCKER, Superintendent.**

*Above left:* **Chinese crews at work on the 90-foot-high Secrettown trestle in the Sierra.**

*Left:* **A tea carrier brings tea to a Chinese work gang drilling Tunnel No 8, 105 miles east of Sacramento.**

*Top:* **Central Pacific patrons view the progress of the trans-Sierra tracks from an excursion train in 1867.**

*Above:* **Central Pacific's first official timetable, published when the railroad began service to Newcastle in 1864.**

record; men who weren't maimed in nitroglycerine mishaps ran the risk of freezing. Strobridge recalled that 'In many instances our camps were carried away by snowslides, and men were buried and many of them were not found until the snow melted the next summer. In the spring of each year the men were taken back from the Truckee River [at a lower elevation on the east side, where work continued year round] into the mountains and an average depth of ten or twelve feet of snow was cleared away before grading could be commenced.

'The total snowfall for the season was about 40 feet, and the depth of hard settled snow was about 18 feet on a level in Summit Valley and Donner Pass, over which we hauled on sleds: track material for forty miles of railroad, three locomo-

tives and forty cars from Cisco to Donner Lake where all was reloaded on wagons and hauled over miry roads to Truckee, a total distance of 28 miles, at enormous cost.' The federal government bonds – $48,000 a mile – were being sold, but construction costs were running at least twice that.

The summit tunnel was completed at last in August 1867, but it took another 11 months before the railroad was completed over the Sierra. Meanwhile, the Union Pacific was easily traversing the plains.

## The Dash to Promontory
In July 1868, the Central Pacific had finally broken out of the mountains, and Charlie Crocker stared in relief and anticipation at the relative flatness of Nevada. The 150-mile crossing

*Left:* **Rail layers place track in Nevada for the gangs of Chinese workers to space and spike during 1868.**

*Top:* **Water had to be hauled to the construction site on the Humboldt Desert, 325 miles east of Sacramento.**

*Above:* **A record 10 miles of track was laid across the Utah desert by the Central Pacific crews on 28 April.**

from Newcastle had taken the railroad 41 months. They crossed the 555 miles to Salt Lake in 10.

The final mad dash was on. Both railroads wanted to reach the lake first, and Leland Stanford personally made five trips to Salt Lake City to expedite the process. The Central Pacific crews, meanwhile, were laying more than a mile of track each day. The question of where they would meet was one of speed, until Congress stepped in on 10 April 1869 and dictated that 'The common terminal of the Union Pacific and Central Pacific railroads shall be at or near Ogden . . . and the Central Pacific Railroad Company shall pay for and own the railroad from the terminus aforesaid to Promontory Summit [north of Salt Lake], at which point the rails shall meet and connect and form one continuous line.'

In the meantime, the Union Pacific's chief engineer, General G M Dodge, was making a great deal out of his 'Irish terriers' having laid six miles of track in a single day. On 28 April 1869, Strobridge invited Dodge to have a look at what his Central Pacific crews could do. A train stood by before daybreak with two miles of rails, and the Central Pacific gangs went to work. Before dawn, the two miles were down. In one instance 240 feet were laid in one minute and 15 seconds. By the end of the day, two million pounds of rails were spiked, gauged and bolted. There were 10 miles and 56 feet of track laid that day, more than had ever been laid, or would ever be laid again, in so short a time. As General Dodge looked on, a Central Pacific locomotive rolled back and forth over the section.

*Below:* On 10 May 1869, Central Pacific's *Jupiter* and Union Pacific's *No 119* came face to face at Promontory, Utah, to celebrate the momentous occasion of a completed transcontinental railroad.

*Below right:* An annual pass signed by E B Crocker and issued in 1868 to J J Orr.

## The Golden Spike

**1862** President Lincoln signs the Pacific Railroad Act, authorizing the Central Pacific to build the western segment of the transcontinental.

**1863** Ground is broken in Sacramento for the Central Pacific on 8 January. The first Central Pacific locomotive, *Governor Stanford*, arrives to go into service. Theodore Judah dies in New York on 2 November.

**1864** The first Central Pacific trains for public travel begin operation between Sacramento and Newcastle on 3 June.

**1865** Ground is broken for the Union Pacific on 5 November. The first Central Pacific ferry service begins on San Francisco Bay.

**1866** Central Pacific construction crews work three shifts a day, battling snowstorms in the Sierra.

**1867** Central Pacific crews continue to battle the elements in the high Sierra during the second consecutive severe winter. First Central Pacific snowsheds are built in the Sierra.

**1868** The Central Pacific completes tracks across the Sierra. The Big Four buy the Southern Pacific on 25 September.

**1869** The Central Pacific crews lay 10 miles of track in a single day on 28 April. The Central Pacific meets the Union Pacific at Promontory on 10 May. Transcontinental freight service is inaugurated on 15 May. The first Silver Palace cars arrive in Sacramento on 4 June. The Central Pacific line from Sacramento to Oakland via Lathrop is completed on 8 November.

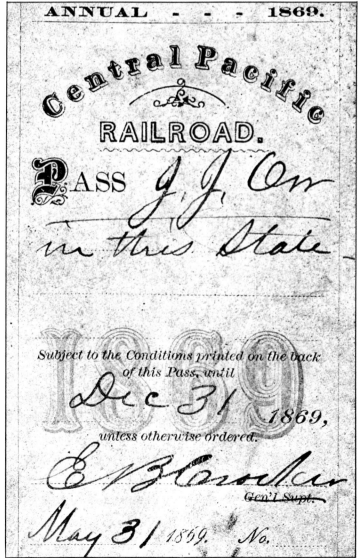

*Below:* Workers and dignitaries gather at Promontory to witness Union Pacific's Thomas Durant and Central Pacific's Leland Stanford drive the ceremonial gold and silver spikes that marked completion of the railroad.

As the sun set on those 10 miles of track and the hundreds that preceded it, the end was very near at hand. On 10 May 1869, the Central Pacific locomotive *Jupiter* moved toward Promontory pulling the private car of Leland Stanford. On the track ahead was the Union Pacific's *No 119* and its vice-president, T C Durant. Stanford had actually arrived on 8 May and had waited in the rain for two days while Durant was delayed. (His train had been kidnapped by some unpaid contractors and was held until the account was settled.)

The rain stopped as the two locomotives paused within sight of one another, and the last rail was put into place. This was followed by speeches and the presentation of a golden railroad spike to Governor Stanford. Nevada offered a silver spike and a speech, and Arizona presented a gold, silver and iron spike and another speech. Stanford responded with a speech. In place of the silver spade he had taken up in Sacramento six years before, he brandished a silver hammer. Telegraph lines that had been strung parallel to the two railroads were poised to carry the news east to Omaha and Chicago, and west to Sacramento and San Francisco. Both the spike and the hammer were wired into the telegraph so the moment of their contact could send a tiny spark of electricity exploding across the nation, poised breathless for this monumental occasion.

A hush fell over the assembled crowd as Leland Stanford swung the silver hammer at the first gold spike. The hammer

plunged downward toward the final notch in the steel belt that would bind the nation ... and missed. Stanford's second blow connected, but it was anticlimatic. Having seen the first blow fall short, a telegraph technician had tapped his key and the celebrations in Chicago and San Francisco had already begun.

*Jupiter* moved forward the last few feet of the 690-mile distance from Sacramento, while *No 119* inched ahead on the last of its 1086-mile trek from Omaha. As their cow-catchers clanged together, the champagne flowed and the Central Pacific and Union Pacific construction superintendents were photographed shaking hands. The gold and silver spikes were unceremoniously pulled, returned to Stanford and replaced with steel ones. Judah's dream had opened the way to the fruition of a whole nation's dreams.

**Above: Leland Stanford drove the last gold spike to join the Union Pacific to the Central Pacific. Representatives of the two were supposed to meet on 8 May, but Union Pacific's *No 119* was two days late.**

**Below: Central Pacific's *Jupiter* heads east carrying Governor Stanford to Promontory in 1869. Near Great Salt Lake in Utah, it paused to meet one last wagon train bound for California on the Overland Route.**

# The Golden State
## 1870-1890

The changes wrought by completion of the trans-continental were far-reaching and immediate. Less than a week after Leland Stanford's parlor car receded across the desert toward the Sierra and Sacramento, the first regularly scheduled freight service from Chicago to Sacramento was inaugurated, on 15 May 1869. The West may not yet have been won, but it had certainly been served notice.

The first Silver Palace sleeping cars, built by Jackson and Sharp of Wilmington, Delaware, arrived in Sacramento on 4 June 1869. The train then moved on to Alameda, across the bay from San Francisco, arriving just six and one-half days after it had pulled out of New York. The Silver Palace cars, with their handsome appointments, served on the Central Pacific until 1883. A typical transcontinental 'hotel' train of 1870 included three Pullman Palace parlor and sleeping cars, four Central Pacific Silver Palace sleeping cars (all with access to a dining car), two regular passenger cars (with no dining-car access) and a baggage car. They were pulled by either Central or Union Pacific locomotives; the two companies made the locomotive exchange at Ogden. The trains left Sacramento every Wednesday for the 133-hour journey to Chicago.

The locomotives used on the Central Pacific were generally distinguishable from their eastern cousins by their large balloon stacks, designed for wood-burning boilers, which were in contrast to the thin stacks of the coal-burning Union Pacific locomotives. While the Union Pacific designation system generally ran toward simply numbering locomotives, the Central Pacific in the early days favored naming as well as numbering them. The first Central Pacific locomotive, *Governor Stanford*, was followed by such colorful successors as *Blue Bird, Diana, Flyer, Goliath, Growler, Hercules, Juno, Magpie, Sampson, Sultana,* the famous *Jupiter* and no fewer than five colors of *Fox*.

***Right:*** **A group of Central Pacific workers warily eye the photographer outside the Sacramento Shops in 1889.**

***Below:*** **Leland Stanford's private car was built at the Central Pacific Railroad Car Works in Sacramento in 1882.**

## Expanding the Network

While the building of the transcontinental consumed most of Central Pacific's attention during its first eight years, the Big Four were also busy putting together an empire within their home state. The Sacramento Valley Rail Road that Theodore Judah completed in 1856 was only the first of many. A number of other railroads were chartered in California in the decade following the start-up of the SVRR, and many of these were actually built. It was toward these that the Big Four turned when their vision shifted to expansion. According to William Hood, a chief engineer of the Central Pacific and an admirer of the Big Four, 'After succeeding in building the Central Pacific, instead of being financially wrecked as freely predicted, and as they themselves feared, the ambition seized the four Associates to build a great system of railroads to develop the Pacific Coast. It is inevitable in such a case that a monopoly for a time of ownership of railroads was necessarily created, and the only way to prevent it was for the Associates to stop building railroads. California would have been many years longer without a complete railroad if these associates had failed to devote their energies and to continually risk their fortunes in railroad construction.'

One of the major railroads in the state, eyed by the Big Four, was the San Francisco & San Jose, which had begun service between the two cities in 1864. Because San Francisco is located at the northern end of a peninsula, any attempt to link it by rail to Sacramento in the northeast (and hence to the nation) would necessarily have to be via San Jose to the south.

Another road of interest to the four associates in Sacramento existed largely on paper, but they owned the land grants to build south from San Francisco and San Jose to Los Angeles and San Diego. This road, which had been organized in 1865 by some of the same San Francisco financiers who had earlier turned down participation in the Central Pacific, was the original Southern Pacific Railroad.

The Southern Pacific had received notice from Congress on 27 July 1866 that it would be the western link of a second transcontinental line then under consideration. On 4 February 1868, the Southern Pacific bought the San Francisco & San Jose Railroad coveted by the Big Four, and

*Left:* **A work train hauls a contractor's flatcars and steam shovel on temporary tracks in Auburn, California.**

*Below:* **Workers at Wadsworth, Nevada, pose around the *Goliath* in 1880. The engine was broken up in 1905.**

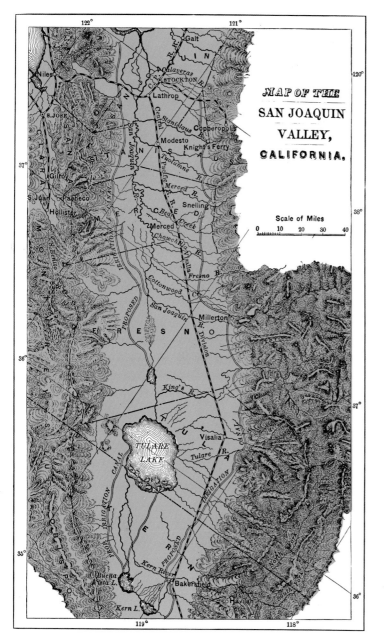

**MAP OF THE**

**SAN JOAQUIN**

**VALLEY,**

**CALIFORNIA.**

Scale of Miles

0    10    20    30    40

in August 1868 Southern Pacific President Timothy Guy Phelps announced his intention to start building his line south to San Diego, where it would then turn east to 'the California line, and to the Mississippi River.'

On 25 September 1869, the Big Four purchased the Southern Pacific. The following year the Central and Southern Pacific operations were merged, although a full merger did not take place for another 15 years, at which time the operations of the entire network came under the Southern Pacific name.

## Putting California on the Map

As the decade of the 1860s ended and the 1870s began, the Big Four owned the beginnings of the network of steel that would ultimately turn California into an economic power-house. They owned the Central Pacific that crossed the state at its midsection. They owned the Yuba Railroad that ran into northern California from Sacramento, and their Central Pacific spur was being built south from Sacramento into the rich San Joaquin Valley. The four owned a San Francisco connection with the lines of the Southern Pacific, which they built to the south as originally planned. It was the beginning of what Frank Norris would call 'the octopus' in his less than complimentary 1901 novel of the same name.

While some saw the empire built by the Big Four as a vicious 'iron-hearted' monster that stifled economic development and political reform in California through graft and corruption, it was also a creator of jobs and a provider of the transportation needed to develop the state's awesome agricultural potential. By 1870, after two decades of gold rush, the mining industry had dissipated. The boom towns became ghost towns as the reality of family farms replaced the dream of finding the mother lode. The railroad had created the potential for basic changes in the fabric of life. Just a few years earlier, a man coming to California faced months of hardship just getting there, and he almost certainly left his family behind. In 1870 he could bring them to the Golden State in less than a week. The Central Pacific encouraged the settlers by offering low passenger fares and by selling off parts of its government land grants at reasonable rates to settlers.

*Above:* **Construction of the San Joaquin Valley Line began in 1869, linking Los Angeles to San Francisco in 1876.**

*Below:* **A celery crop is harvested at the Stillwater Orchards Company in the heart of the San Joaquin Valley.**

The Central Pacific/Southern Pacific developed marketing programs and devoted their resources to encouraging immigration. The men picked to head these programs clearly had the state's best interests at heart. Southern Pacific's first chief land agent, Benjamin Redding, was a former secretary of state, patron of the Academy of Sciences and regent of the University of California. His successor, William Mills, who served from 1883 to 1907, was an agriculture reformer and leader of the antihydraulic mining movement and the Yosemite Park Commission. The Southern Pacific was one of the biggest promoters of bringing Sequoia and Yosemite into the national park system.

Land agent Mills was also a strong promoter of agricultural diversity. With the support of the Big Four, he promoted the notion of a variety of specialty crops to maximize the advantage of California's many climatic regions. As a result the San Joaquin Valley became one of the richest agricultural areas in the world. As Huntington observed, 'The many advantages of climate and soil which the State of California offers settlers are becoming better known each year.'

The popular notion has it that the railroads of the West, particularly the Southern Pacific, held on to their government land grants for the purpose of speculation. Generally speaking, the opposite was true. The Big Four could see more value in allowing the land to be owned at reasonable cost by people who would ultimately use the railroads to transport their products.

*Below:* **The *San Mateo* hauls a passenger train over the old San Francisco & San Jose line, which was completed in 1864.**

## The Golden State

**1865** San Francisco businessmen under Timothy Phelps found the Southern Pacific Railroad to build a San Francisco-to-San Diego line.

**1868** The Big Four buy the Southern Pacific on 25 September.

**1869** The Central Pacific meets the Union Pacific at Promontory on 10 May, opens service to Oakland via Lathrop on 8 November and begins construction on a San Joaquin Valley line on 31 December.

**1870** The Big Four merge the Central Pacific and the Southern Pacific operationally, having purchased a San Francisco-to-San Jose line in 1868.

**1872** Central Pacific/Southern Pacific lines in the San Joaquin Valley are completed, as is the line north to Redding. The Big Four found the Occidental & Oriental Steamship Company. The first locomotive is built at Southern Pacific's Sacramento Shops.

**1873** Central Pacific/Southern Pacific general offices are moved to Fourth and Townsend in San Francisco. The Coast Line reaches Soledad and the Valley Line reaches Delano.

**1874** Southern Pacific reaches Bakersfield on 8 November and work begins on the Tehachapi Loop.

**1876** The Tehachapi Loop is completed. Charles Crocker pounds the golden spike near Palmdale to symbolize opening of the San Francisco-to-Los Angeles line, with the first through-train arriving in Los Angeles on 5 September. Southern Pacific sends a special train to the Centennial Exposition to publicize Californian agriculture.

## San Francisco, Hub of an Empire

When Leland Stanford slammed the golden spike into the tie at Promontory, San Francisco was already a world-class metropolis. Separated though she was from the rest of the nation by 2000 miles, she had developed a cultural milieu that shared in the best that the world had to offer. San Francisco's emporiums displayed the latest from Europe and New York, as well as treasures from the Orient. It was in part because of her isolation that she thrived. Her factories, including such locomotive builders as the Vulcan Iron Works, throbbed, and her theaters proliferated. Her population exceeded that of Hong Kong or Frankfurt. The Palace Hotel on Market Street came to be known as one of the world's grandest hostelries. A pearl without peer in the western wilderness, fueled by the wealth of silver and gold mines, San Francisco became the financial capital of the West, a title to which she can still lay claim more than a century later.

It was to this magnificent metropolis that the Big Four inevitably came. The headquarters of the Central Pacific/Southern Pacific empire was established at Fourth and Townsend streets, near the bustling and expanding railhead that remains today a principal Southern Pacific yard. The San Francisco station was built a block away at Third Street, where it remained for 103 years. The Big Four also expanded into shipping. In 1872 they started the Occidental & Oriental Steamship Company to develop trade with the Far East. They purchased 60 acres of San Francisco's waterfront, and through the O & O they dominated the city's port activity and her foreign trade for the next 20 years. Meanwhile, the rail-

road came to control the passenger ferries between Oakland and San Francisco, with terminals at each also controlled by the Big Four.

At that time, as today, the grandest addresses in San Francisco were at the top of Nob Hill. For prestige, Nob Hill rivaled New York's Fifth Avenue, and for views it exceeded Fifth Avenue a hundredfold. The cream of Western society lived on Nob Hill, and it was only natural that the wealthy newcomers from Sacramento should gravitate there. Both Leland Stanford and Charles Crocker immediately undertook construction of grand palaces on Nob Hill, the likes of which even San Francisco had not yet seen. Company engineers were brought in to design the type of foundations that would permit the splendid homes to perch on the precipitous cliffs. The Stanford mansion rose at the southwest corner of California and Powell Streets, and Charlie Crocker selected a site two blocks away on the northwest corner of California and Taylor streets.

However, Mark Hopkins, whose wealth could have easily afforded a home on the grandest scale, chose a residence more in keeping with his less flamboyant style. A vegetarian, he rented a small cottage on Sutter Street near Leavenworth, where he could grow vegetables in the backyard. The introspective Hopkins spent the rest of his life in this rented

*Left:* A view of San Francisco, looking east from the corner of Powell and California streets.

*Below left:* Southern Pacific's General Offices on the corner of Fourth and Townsend, as they appeared in 1887.

*Above:* Charlie Crocker built a showplace of a home on Nob Hill that cost a mere $1,500,000 to construct.

*Below:* Mark Hopkins' Nob Hill home, unfinished when he died, later became the San Francisco Art Institute.

**Above:** Leland Stanford *(pictured at right)* built the California Street Cable Railroad that ran from Market Street near the water up California Street to Nob Hill. This is the view looking down California Street from the top of the hill.

**Below:** Annual passes issued to Jennie Stanford and signed by Leland Stanford in 1882.

cottage, tending his garden and walking daily to work at the company offices on Townsend Street. Principally to indulge his wife, Hopkins did consent to the construction of a Nob Hill chateau, but it was yet to be completed when he died.

C P Huntington, who rarely frequented the West Coast, generally held court at the Palace Hotel when he was in town. However, he eventually did purchase a home on Nob Hill, which he did not use until the last decade of the century, when he served as president of Southern Pacific. The mansion he bought, across Taylor Street from Crocker's house, once belonged to General David Douty Colton. The general, whose title derived from a short affiliation with the state militia, had become so closely associated with the Big Four that they were briefly referred to in the press as the 'Big Four and a half.' The general died in October 1878, the victim of what was rumored to be murder, but was never proved.

While the Southern Pacific was building the railroads whose steam trains would provide the transportation to unify the state, other entrepreneurs were building the rail lines whose cable-driven trains would unify the city of San Francisco. The city's first cable railway, the Clay Street Hill Railroad, began service on 1 August 1873, hauling passengers from the Clay Street hill on Kearny Street to Jones. Not to be outdone, Leland Stanford put together a consortium that included Crocker, Colton, Hopkins and Louis Sloss to build a competing line. Known as the California Street Cable Railroad, the line opened in 1878, running from Market Street to the mansions atop Nob Hill via California Street. The original route survives today as the California Street Cable Car Line of the San Francisco Municipal Railway.

### The Empire Expands

With their base firmly grounded in San Francisco, the Big Four spread their empire throughout the state. By 1873, the year that Southern Pacific headquarters were established in

*Left:* The *Grey Eagle* was the first locomotive of the Central Pacific assigned to full-time fire-train duty.

*Below:* The *Solano* departs from Port Costa, carrying passengers and trains south to Oakland or San Francisco. One of the original Central Pacific ferryboats, *Solano* was placed into service on 28 December 1879 to link rail lines from the north with lines from the south and east.

*Above:* On 19 August 1887 crowds gathered at the State Street Station to greet Southern Pacific's first train to Santa Barbara in Southern California.

*Below:* Locomotive *No 73* of the Big Four's Southern Pacific fleet on the turntable at the Monterey roundhouse in 1887.

Railroad mileage of the Southern Pacific Company in 1884, at the time of its creation through a merger of the Central Pacific Railroad Company and the Southern Pacific Railroad Company.

| | | |
|---|---:|---:|
| Southern Pacific Railroad | | 1306.90 |
| Southern Pacific Northern Division | 202.50 | |
| Southern Pacific of California | 552.85 | |
| Southern Pacific of Arizona | 384.25 | |
| Southern Pacific of New Mexico | 167.30 | |
| | | |
| Central Pacific Railroad | | 1254.24 |
| Galveston, Harrisburg & Antonio Railway | | 936.74 |
| Morgan's Louisiana & Texas Railroad | | 281.00 |
| Mexican International Railroad | | 171.00 |
| Northern Railway | | 153.63 |
| California Pacific Railroad | | 115.44 |
| Louisiana Western Railroad | | 112.00 |
| Texas & New Orleans Railroad | | 105.10 |
| Sabine & East Texas Railroad | | 104.00 |
| Stockton & Copperopolis Railroad | | 49.00 |
| San Pablo & Tulare Railroad | | 46.51 |
| Los Angeles & San Diego Railroad | | 27.60 |
| Amador Branch Railroad | | 27.20 |
| Los Angeles & Independence Railroad | | 16.83 |
| Berkeley Branch Railroad | | 3.84 |
| | | |
| Total system mileage | | 4711.03 |

**Above:** Section men turn out for work near the entrance to the San Fernando tunnel in the San Fernando Mountains north of Los Angeles in 1875, when the Southern Pacific was extending its line south from the San Joaquin Valley to Los Angeles. Construction was finished in 1876.

San Francisco, rails had been laid as far north as Redding. Construction of the Central Pacific's San Joaquin Valley Line (originally the San Joaquin Valley Rail Road) had laid out such cities as Fresno and had pushed as far south as Delano, while Southern Pacific's Coast Line had reached Soledad.

In November 1874 Southern Pacific reached Bakersfield and its engineers, under chief engineer Bill Hood, had designed the Tehachapi Loop to conquer the last mountainous obstacle on the route south to Los Angeles, the City of the Angels. As crews attacked the Tehachapi Mountains from the north, other crews were building the Southern Pacific line out of Los Angeles. On 5 September 1876, at Palmdale, in a scene reminiscent of the one at Promontory five years before, Charlie Crocker drove another golden spike and the Golden State was united from north to south. A Southern Pacific train bound from San Francisco reached Los Angeles the same day. Fulfilling the dream of Southern Pacific's original founders, the Big Four immediately turned east from Los Angeles, reaching the Colorado River across from Fort Yuma, Arizona, in May 1877. Yuma was an important linchpin in their grand design to defeat Tom Scott's Texas Pacific Railroad in the race for domination of the Southwest.

The Big Four also continued to expand their empire by purchasing smaller railroads. In 1876 they bought the California Pacific, which had been operating a line between Sacramento and Benicia, a city near the point where the Sacramento River enters San Francisco Bay. The line was particularly valuable because it was level, without complicating hills or grades. The California Pacific also operated a train ferry from South Vallejo near Benicia down to Oakland, where the Big Four already dominated ferry service across the bay to San Francisco.

By 1884 the empire consisted of no less than every mile of standard-gauge railroad in the state of California, a 4711-mile system radiating from the bustling San Francisco yards to the far corners of the state and 800 miles beyond. By that same year, the Central Pacific itself, nearly broke when the spike was driven at Promontory, had grossed $277 million, with a profit of roughly $37 million.

*Below:* An old Southern Pacific passenger train at the Monterey Station in about 1882. Southern Pacific opened the famous Del Monte Lodge four years later to attract visitors to the Monterey Bay area.

*Right:* When the thrifty, reclusive Mark Hopkins died in 1878, he was one of the richest men in the world.

## A New Kentucky Home

The Southern Pacific Company came into being in 1884 as a new corporation, a holding company for such entities as the Southern Pacific Railroad Company and the Central Pacific. The company was incorporated on 17 March 1884 in the state of Kentucky; none of its rail lines ran there, but Kentucky limited the liability of a company's stockholders and allowed it to increase its capital stock without state permission. It was from Kentucky that the Southern Pacific Company officially leased its historic ancestor, the Central Pacific Railroad, on 17 February 1885.

The company home remained in Kentucky for 63 years, paying a nominal $100,000 in annual taxes, until the state suddenly reassessed the property and delivered a $20-million bill for back taxes in 1947. The company moved that same year to the safety of Delaware, another state where there were no Southern Pacific rails, but in which the financial climate was to prove better than in Kentucky.

## Whither the Big Four

Cracks had begun to appear in the edifice that was the Big Four even before the move to San Francisco. Charlie Crocker actually sold out to his partners in 1871, but returned two years later with the move to San Francisco and remained there until his death. He died on 14 August 1888 at the fabulous Del Monte Lodge, a huge resort complex that the company had built to help attract tourists to the Monterey Peninsula south of San Francisco. His place at the Southern Pacific table was taken by his son, Charles Frederick Crocker, and the remnants of his family empire are still in evidence in

California. The Crocker Bank is now one of California's four largest, and the firm of H S Crocker is one of San Francisco's leading stationers.

Crocker was actually preceded in death by the frail Mark Hopkins. The eldest of the Four died on 29 March 1878 in his car on a siding near Yuma, Arizona, where he had gone to observe the Southern Pacific's progress in the Southwest. He left a fortune valued at roughly $25 million, an unfinished Nob Hill mansion and the wife for whom he had reluctantly consented to build this opulent home. At 45, Mary Sherwood Hopkins was 20 years younger than her husband had been, and she had no intention of prolonging the reclusive life she had lived at his side. She finished the Nob Hill mansion, probably the gaudiest of Nob Hill homes, and became the toast of San Francisco, and later New York, society. At the age of 50 she initiated a bitter dispute with adopted son Timothy Hopkins when she married a 28-year-old interior decorator named Edward Searles. Because of the feud, it was Searles, not the younger Hopkins, who inherited Mark's fortune when she died in 1891. Searles, meanwhile, had been taken under the wing of Collis Huntington and continued to vote his Southern Pacific shares in Huntington's favor even after Timothy Hopkins sued successfully for a substantial part of his stepfather's wealth.

Unlike his associates, Leland Stanford enjoyed the Southern Pacific and was the only one who never seriously entertained thoughts of selling out. Though Huntington was the power behind the Big Four, he was in New York while Stanford was in San Francisco, in the president's chair. From that chair at Fourth and Townsend, and from his elaborate

## The Golden State

**1877**  Southern Pacific lines reach and cross the Colorado River.

**1878**  Mark Hopkins dies in Yuma, Arizona, on 29 March.

**1879**  The first experimental use of an oil-burning locomotive takes place on Southern Pacific lines.

**1880**  The Big Four minus Mark Hopkins purchase the Pacific Mail Transpacific Steamship line and integrate it into the Central Pacific holdings.

**1883**  Southern Pacific lines reach the Colorado River at Needles, California, meeting the Atchison, Topeka & Santa Fe Railroad. William Mills becomes Southern Pacific's chief land agent.

**1884**  Southern Pacific is incorporated in Kentucky on 17 March.

**1885**  The Southern Pacific Railroad Company and the Central Pacific Railroad Company are joined under a single holding company called the Southern Pacific Company on 17 February. Southern Pacific takes over all operations on 1 April. Leland Stanford is elected to the US Senate, and has a serious break in relations with C P Huntington.

**1886**  The Del Monte Hotel, the most famous of many Southern Pacific resorts, opens in Monterey, California. The first Southern Pacific refrigerator cars are put into service.

**1887**  The Southern Pacific and the Atchison, Topeka & Santa Fe engage in a rate war, cutting colonist fares to California. The first Southern Pacific train reaches Santa Barbara on 19 August. Continuous service to Portland, Oregon, is opened on 17 December. Southern Pacific takes control of the Southern Pacific Coast Railroad between Felton (Santa Cruz County) and Oakland.

**1888**  A special promotional train, 'California on Wheels,' is sent to the Midwest to exhibit and promote the products of Southern Pacific's service area. The arcade station opens in Los Angeles. Charles Crocker dies at the Del Monte Hotel in Monterey on 14 August.

**1889**  The Southern Pacific Colonization Agency is formed to help settle small farmers on railroad land.

**1890**  Sequoia National Park is established with strong support from Southern Pacific. The Southern Pacific presidency passes from Leland Stanford to C P Huntington.

**1893**  Leland Stanford dies in Palo Acto on 21 June.

Nob Hill home, Stanford became one of the central fixtures of San Francisco life. He presided over not only the West's biggest railroad, but the bay ferries and one of the city's street railroads as well. He was even president of the Pacific Telegraph Company, where Frank Jaynes of Western Union fame was a junior partner.

While Leland Stanford was the center of San Francisco life, the center of Leland Stanford's life was his son and heir, Leland Stanford, Jr. Young Leland was born in 1868, after his father and Jane Lathrop had been married for 18 years. The boy matured into a young man of uncommon brilliance. By the time he reached his teens, he was literate beyond his years and capable of conversing intelligently on a broad range of topics from literature to science. He had a superb collection of Egyptian antiquities and had even designed several types of steam engine. He was also a thoughtful and attentive boy, and his respect and admiration for his father was exceeded only by his father's admiration for him. His future with his father's company seemed assured, and had it actually come to pass, the company's future would have been enhanced even beyond what it actually achieved.

The tenure of Leland Stanford, Jr at the helm of the empire never became a reality. On 13 March 1884, while on his second trip to Europe with his parents, he sickened and died at the Hotel Bristol in Florence, Italy. He was 16 years of age. As a monument to his son, Leland Stanford intended to establish a memorial technical school at the University of California. When the state denied him an appointment to the university's Board of Regents, he started his own university near his farm in Palo Alto, south of San Francisco. Today Leland Stanford, Jr University stands as one of the leading institutions of higher learning in the nation.

Following the death of his only son, Stanford returned to politics. His decision to run for the US Senate in 1885 probably had the net result of destroying what was left of his relationship with Huntington, the only other surviving member of the original Big Four.

The term of Senator James Farley expired on 3 March 1885. His replacement was to be selected by the Republican-dominated state assembly, so the candidate of that party was expected to be the nominee. The Southern Pacific and, of course, both Huntington and Stanford, were supporting Congressman Aaron Sargent, who had been a loyal supporter of railroad interests in Congress. At the last minute, Stanford's name was entered into consideration by the caucusing state assemblymen. Huntington, who had pledged the company's support to Sargent, was furious. Stanford was selected and from then on he naturally spent most of his time in Washington. He was company president in name only.

*Left:* C P Huntington replaced Leland Stanford as president of the Southern Pacific in 1890. Huntington had forced his associate into a showdown for the top job after several years as de facto president.

*Below:* The *Governor Stanford*, Central Pacific's locomotive *No 1*, heads into the Stanford Museum in 1916.

*Bottom:* Charles Crocker married Mary Deming in 1852 and had three sons and a daughter. After his death, son Charles Frederick took over control of his shares in the Southern Pacific.

*Left:* The locomotive *Gorilla* at the Rocklin, California, roundhouse in 1869.

*Far left:* The huge 14-wheeled *El Gobernador* was intended to replace the less powerful 8-wheeled engines.

On 28 February 1890, Stanford and Huntington met in New York with representatives of the Crocker, Hopkins and Searles interests. It was decided that Collis P Huntington, de facto president for the past five years, should replace Stanford as president. A strictly ceremonial 'executive committee' was then established, with Stanford to serve as its ceremonial chairman. With this restructuring, the center of gravity within the Southern Pacific Company officially shifted from Stanford to Huntington and from San Francisco to New York. Leland Stanford was elected to a second senatorial term in 1891, but he spent most of the next two years on the farm in Palo Alto, where he died on 21 June 1893.

## The Early Locomotives

The first four locomotives used on the Central Pacific were the *Governor Stanford* (*No 1*), *Pacific* (*No 2*), *C P Huntington* (*No 3*) and *T D Judah* (*No 4*). Typical of the early series is the *C P Huntington,* which later became Southern Pacific's *No 1* and which is preserved in the California Railroad Museum in Sacramento. It is 29.5 feet long and has a 4-2-2 wheel layout, that is, a four-wheel truck, one pair of drive wheels and two trailing wheels. The 21.75-ton *Huntington* was capable of pulling four times its own weight, and had a top speed of 35 mph and a speed of 15 mph on a grade of 26 feet per mile. Central Pacific *No 6,* the *Conness,* was the first locomotive ordered by the company solely to haul freight. It was a big 4-6-0, 52 feet long (with tender) and weighing 60 tons (tender included). Built by William Mason of Taunton, Massachusetts, in 1865, it could pull 18 freight cars.

The expense and delay involved in hauling locomotives by ship around Cape Horn led the Big Four to decide very early on to set up a locomotive factory of their own in Sacramento. The first locomotive built there was Central Pacific *No 173,* in 1872. The early locomotives built by the Central Pacific Sacramento Shops in 1872 and 1873 were American type 4-4-0s, 52 feet long and weighing 33 tons fully loaded. The Sacramento Shops produced over 200 locomotives over the years, the last one rolling out in 1937.

While the earliest few Central Pacific locomotives weighed in at 18 to 22 tons, most of those delivered by the late 1870s weighed between 47 and 50 tons. The major parts of the Sacramento-built locomotives, as well as the engine frames, were made of wrought iron until about 1874, when steel came into use for these components. The boilers were of plate iron, the firebox of plate copper and the steam flues of brass. Bumpers and pilots were made of wood until as late as the early 1880s.

In 1884 the Sacramento Shops built what was the largest locomotive in the world, to haul loads over the Tehachapi Mountains in Southern California. Built specifically at the request of Leland Stanford, *El Gobernador* weighed 73 tons alone or 194.5 tons with a fully loaded tender. Engine and tender were 65 feet, 5 inches long and were considered too big for turntables and many bridges; they had to be disassembled and hauled to the base of the Tehachapis as freight. The boiler was too small, and *El Gobernador* was a failure. Hauled back to Sacramento for a rebuilding that never took place, the big locomotive was cut up for scrap in 1894.

*Above:* Locomotive *No 1212*, a 'monkey hog,' was built by the Globe Locomotive Works of South Boston in 1868 and sold to Folsom Prison in 1900, where it was photographed. Two convicts escaped by hiding in its water tank. In 1968, country singer Johnny Cash released the song *Folsom Prison Blues* about a convict listening to the lonesome wail of a train whistle.

*Above right:* Locomotive *No 380*, also a monkey hog, was the first Southern Pacific freight train to be equipped with Westinghouse automatic air brakes.

*Below:* This Stevens monkey, locomotive *No 123*, was built in Southern Pacific's Sacramento Shops in 1886.

In 1885, the same year that the Central Pacific and the Southern Pacific merged, General Master Mechanic A J Stevens was made responsible for designing as well as building most of the locomotives to come out of the Sacramento Shops. Through 1888, all of the Sacramento-built locomotives were Stevens designed. Stevens is most noted for his valve gears, which were commonly referred to as 'monkey motions,' because the return rods had the appearance of a monkey hopping along when the locomotive was in motion. The first four 'monkey hogs' (trains that had Stevens valve gears) were 4-4-0s weighing 26.4 tons, delivered in 1886 for passenger service. These were followed in 1888 by 12 more 4-4-0 monkeys with larger boilers. Between 1886 and 1887, there were 21 4-6-0 monkey hogs built in Sacramento. They were 56 feet long, and each weighed 87.5 tons with its tender. They had the familiar balloon stack common to locomotives with wood-burning boilers, but were retrofitted with straight stacks when coal came into common use as a fuel on the Southern Pacific. The next block of 10 monkey hogs were 2-8-0s delivered in 1888, the first of that wheel layout in Southern Pacific service. They weighed 92.5 tons (with tender) and had twice the tractive power of the earlier monkeys.

Coal was used as a fuel on Southern Pacific lines for a relatively shorter time than on other railroads. Oil was used experimentally for the first time in the 4-4-0 locomotive *Young America* in 1879, at a time when large-scale conversion from wood to coal had yet to take place. Wood-burning locomotives were still being built in Sacramento in the late 1880s, and oil was first used operationally in 1895, so the era of coal as the dominant fuel was short on most of the Southern Pacific routes. The Los Angeles and Sacramento divisions converted to oil in 1901 and 1902, respectively. However, the Salt Lake division did not convert fully from coal to oil until 1912.

# The Golden West
## 1870-1890

**T**he Golden State of California may have been the keystone of the Southern Pacific, but it was only part of the empire, an empire that stretched from the Pacific to the southwestern deserts of Arizona and New Mexico, across the great state of Texas, and all the way to New Orleans and the mouth of the Mississippi. To the north, the empire reached into Oregon and came to dominate the rails of that state. The first company steel breached the Colorado River heading eastward toward Texas in 1877, but Texas already had a railroad infrastructure with a history predating the rails of California.

### Rails Across Texas

The first railroad charter to be issued in the Lone Star State came in 1836, when the state was still the Republic of Texas. By the time of statehood nine years later, three railroads had been chartered, but none had been built. In 1851 neither Crocker nor Stanford had yet come to California when work began on the Buffalo Bayou, Brazos & Colorado Railway (BBB&C), the first railroad in Texas and the oldest section of tracks to ultimately become part of the Southern Pacific. The

brainchild of General Sidney Sherman, the BBB&C was only the second railroad to operate west of the Mississippi. By the time Californians were taking their first railroad ride on Theodore Judah's SVRR in 1856, the BBB&C had reached from Houston to the western bank of the Brazos. There were no fewer than 40 railroads in Texas that would eventually come under the Southern Pacific umbrella. Not among these, however, was the Vicksburg & El Paso Railroad, which later became known as the Texas Western, and which in 1856 changed its name to the Southern Pacific Railroad. This Southern Pacific was soon gone, and should not be confused with the giant railroad company of California.

By the time the first transcontinental line was completed at Promontory in 1869, the nation's major railroaders were not interested in the many small regional rail lines in Texas. Their focus was on the idea of a single railroad across the whole state, and the somewhat more distant dream of connecting

**Rails across Texas. The wood-burning locomotive *Stowe* on the disk at the El Paso railhead *(below)* belonged to the Texas & New Orleans Railroad, a Southern Pacific subsidiary. Oil tank cars *(right)* monopolize the Beaumont rail yard.**

*Left:* Once one of the highest bridges in the world, Southern Pacific's bridge over the Pecos River in southwestern Texas was 326 feet high and 1515 feet long. It was shortened from 2180 feet in 1910 and reinforced. The original bridge was opened for traffic in March 1892, when a section of the railroad's original line, built several miles farther south in 1882-83, was abandoned. It was on this abandoned section that the last spike was driven on 12 January 1883, completing the Sunset Route from Los Angeles to New Orleans.

*Below:* The Texas & New Orleans roundhouse in Houston, looking west from Hardy Street before the 1920 fire.

## The Golden West: Rails Across Texas

**1851** Construction begins on the Buffalo Bayou, Brazos & Colorado Railway (BBB&C) between Houston and Alleyton, Texas. The BBB&C is the oldest line to become part of the Southern Pacific.

**1852** Construction begins on the second oldest section of track that would become part of the Southern Pacific: the New Orleans, Opelousas & Great Western Railroad in Louisiana.

**1853** The BBB&C begins service as the first railroad in Texas and the second railroad west of the Mississippi.

**1859** The Texas & New Orleans Railroad, later an important part of Southern Pacific, is chartered in Louisiana.

**1862** The New Orleans, Opelousas & Great Western Railroad is taken over by Union troops and operated as the US Military Railroad (until 1866).

**1870** The BBB&C becomes the Galveston, Harrisburg & San Antonio Railroad.

**1871** The US Congress passes the Texas & Pacific Act authorizing the Texas & Pacific Railroad to build west from Texas to Yuma, Arizona, and the Southern Pacific to build east to Yuma.

**1873** The Texas & Pacific halts construction at Dallas (until 1876).

**1877** The Southern Pacific builds to, and crosses, the Colorado River at Yuma, becoming the first railroad in Arizona. President Hayes signs an executive order on 9 October permitting Southern Pacific to continue to cross Arizona. Jay Gould gains control of the Texas & Pacific. The Galveston, Harrisburg & San Antonio (soon to be part of Southern Pacific) reaches San Antonio.

**1878** Mark Hopkins dies in Yuma, Arizona, on 29 March.

**1880** Construction of the Southern Pacific line reaches Tucson, Arizona, and the first train arrives on 20 March.

**1881** The Southern Pacific line reaches El Paso, Texas, on 19 May and Sierra Blanca on 25 November. Southern Pacific undertakes to build the Galveston, Harrisburg & San Antonio westward from San Antonio, starting on 15 July.

**1883** Southern Pacific crews complete the Pecos River High Bridge. The lines coming east from California and west from San Antonio meet on 12 January at the Pecos River, where the gold spike is driven. The first train from New Orleans reaches San Antonio on 6 February and the first train from Los Angeles reaches San Antonio on 7 February. The Morgan Steamship Line, with service between New Orleans and East Coast ports, is acquired by Southern Pacific.

**1885** The Southern Pacific Railroad Company and the Central Pacific Railroad Company are joined under a single holding company called the Southern Pacific Company on 17 February.

**1888** The Galveston, Harrisburg & San Antonio maintenance shops are merged with those of the Texas & New Orleans and moved to Houston, giving Southern Pacific control of the largest such facilities in the Southwest.

that line with the Pacific coast. In the early 1870s, both Jay Gould of the Union Pacific and C P Huntington of the Central Pacific, flushed with their common victory, found themselves with a mutual goal. In the decade that followed, they turned from the idea of another transcontinental co-operative venture toward the steps that each hoped would make him the one for whom the dream would come true.

The key figure was a Mr Tom Scott, proprietor of the Texas & Pacific (later Texas Pacific) Railroad, to whom Huntington had once tried to sell Southern Pacific during its financial hard times of the early 1870s. Scott had a pocketful of state and federal land grants and a stated objective of building his railroad from Dallas all the way to San Diego via Yuma, Arizona. Scott's westernmost terminus remained at Dallas from 1873 to 1876, when he began again to build across the Texas prairie toward the distant Pacific. The Southern Pacific had just barely completed its line connecting northern and southern California in 1876 when Huntington, like a battlefield commander, ordered his troops to turn east toward Yuma.

After Southern Pacific took Yuma in May 1977, Tom Scott was defeated. Jay Gould took over the Texas Pacific, but in 1880 Huntington and Southern Pacific bought the Galveston, Harrisburg & San Antonio Railroad (GH&SA), whose importance is evident by its route through the cities in its name. The Southern Pacific-owned GH&SA started west from San Antonio in 1881. Jay Gould's Texas Pacific was never built west of Texas.

## The Battle of Yuma
In 1877 Yuma was nothing more than a dusty little desert town in Arizona, adjacent to the US Cavalry's Fort Yuma, but to the great railroad barons it was much more. It was Waterloo, and Huntington was Wellington. Yuma was lifted from obscurity to be the site of a turning point in railroad history that allowed western railroads to expand as they did.

It was the cornerstone of Tom Scott's dream for his Texas Pacific, but he was still 1200 miles away in May 1877, when the Southern Pacific arrived at the western banks of the Colorado River. Some of the Southern Pacific men crossed the river to Yuma, on the Arizona side, armed with a generous supply of whisky that they proposed sharing with the cavalry troopers at Fort Yuma. The cavalry's job was to protect Arizona from the Apaches – and from an incursion by a railroad company that did not have a land grant to build a railroad into Arizona. The initial toasts turned into a bout of merrymaking that lasted nearly a week. By this time, however, a wooden bridge had spanned the Colorado. Southern Pacific was already laying rails when the troops finally were able to shake off enough of the whisky to stop the railroad men. Popular opinion in southwest Arizona, however, was vociferously supportive of the idea of having a railroad serve the area. The Arizona Legislature backed the populace, as did Army Chief of Staff General William Tecumseh Sherman in Washington. Huntington, meanwhile, went to work on President Rutherford B Hayes, who was at last persuaded to sign an executive order on 9 October 1977 authorizing Southern Pacific access to Arizona. The battle of Yuma had been won without firing a shot.

## The Sunset Route
By the time Mark Hopkins died in his private car outside Yuma in March 1878, Southern Pacific tracks had been running across the Arizona desert for nearly nine months. The second transcontinental line was called the Sunset Route: it was all Southern Pacific, from the Mississippi Delta to the Pacific Coast. Building east from Yuma, Southern Pacific crews reached Tucson on 20 March 1880. By 19 May 1881, the railroad had crossed both Arizona and New Mexico and had reached El Paso, Texas. At the same time, the Southern Pacific's GH&SA began building westward from San Antonio.

On 12 January 1883, the two lines finally met on the west bank of the Pecos, 227 miles from San Antonio, and the last

Southern Pacific's coal-burning locomotive *No 3301* near El Paso, Texas. On Southern Pacific trains, oil was used experimentally as a fuel as early as 1879 and by 1895 was being used operationally in place of coal on some lines.

spike was driven by Colonel Tom Pierce, the GH&SA president. The first train from New Orleans arrived in San Antonio on 6 February, and the first train from Los Angeles the next day. C P Huntington, in the meantime, had acquired the Louisiana & Texas Railroad & Steamship Company from Charles Morgan. This not only provided the last link in the Southern Pacific line, connecting Los Angeles to New Orleans, but it gave the company access to eastern ports by means of Morgan steamships. Sunset Route passengers were then able to travel from Los Angeles to New Orleans by rail and on to New York, enjoying '100 golden hours at sea,' as the advertising copy read. The steamship link continued to be an important adjunct to the Sunset Route for more than half a century, until it was permanently discontinued during World War II.

## North to Oregon

Oregon Territory became the state of Oregon in 1859, making it the second state after California to be established in the Far West. It was only natural that some thought should be given to connecting the two by rail. The Central Pacific was only into its fourth year in 1865 when citizens of the city of Marysville, 52 miles north of Sacramento, established the California & Oregon Railroad to build a line north to Portland, Oregon. Construction began, but the company underwent difficulties and was sold and resold several times before it was incorporated into the Central Pacific network in 1870.

In Oregon, Ben Holladay, who had made a fortune in the stagecoach business before selling out to Wells Fargo in 1866, became involved in a scheme to build a railroad south from Portland. The Oregon Central Railroad Company was formed, and on 26 October 1869 construction began. By completing 20 miles before Christmas, the line qualified for a federal subsidy, which allowed it to forge ahead southward through the Willamette Valley. The Oregon Central reached Oregon's capital, Salem, on 29 September 1870 in time to carry visitors to the state fair. The railroad reached Eugene a year later and Roseburg by the end of 1872.

As Holladay pushed his railroad through the Oregon backwoods, he continued to sell bonds to supplement his federal aid and to hope that demand would arise for the service he had established. The demand for a railroad in this remote part of Oregon simply didn't exist, and Holladay's bondholders, mostly German industrialists, seized the company. They turned it over to Henry Villard, who had established a good

*Right:* The Cascade Railroad locomotive *Ann,* built by the Vulcan Iron Works in San Francisco in 1862, worked for the Oregon & California out of Scio, Oregon. Southern Pacific is also reported to have used the engine for branch-line construction in Oregon.

*Below:* A hotel stagecoach and horse-drawn carriages of the Salem Street Railroad Company pause to drop off and collect passengers at the Salem, Oregon, train station in 1892.

*Next page:* This Whitney Timber Company locomotive, at work on a feeder line to Southern Pacific's Tillamook Branch, comprised the rod engine *Big Jack* and the climax-geared engine *Molly O.*

## The Golden West: North to Oregon

**1865** The California & Oregon Railroad is incorporated on 30 June to build a line from Marysville, California (near Sacramento) to Portland, Oregon.

**1868** The Oregon Central Railroad begins building south from Portland in April.

**1869** Ben Holladay's Oregon Central (later Oregon & California) crosses the Clackamas River on 23 December.

**1870** The Oregon & California reaches Salem on 29 September in time for the state fair.

**1871** The Oregon & California continues south through the Willamette Valley, reaching Eugene on 15 October.

**1872** Ben Holladay's Oregon & California goes bankrupt and is taken over by Henry Villard. Central Pacific's California & Oregon reaches north to Redding, California.

**1883** Henry Villard's Northern Pacific reaches Portland.

**1884** Henry Villard's Oregon & California reaches Ashland, Oregon, near the California border.

**1887** The Big Four take control of the Oregon & California when Villard goes bankrupt. The California & Oregon begins to cross the Siskiyous in May. The California & Oregon meets the Oregon & California at Ashland on 17 December. Continuous service is now possible between Portland and all points on the Southern Pacific network.

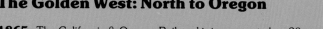

Portland & Willamette Valley Railway Co.

Good for One First-Class Passage.

**OSWEGO** TO **PORTLAND.**

FORM R. E.    Vice President.

*Below:* The Southern Pacific Station in Beaumont, Texas, near the Louisiana border. The line between New Orleans and Los Angeles, the Sunset Route, became operational on 12 January 1883, although Beaumont had been an important rail head for years.

*Top:* This 23 June 1868 ticket for travel between Portland and Ashland, Oregon, on Southern Pacific cost $13.68.

*Above:* A first-class ticket for travel from Lake Oswego to Portland, dated 22 July 1888, aboard a competitive line. Oregon was linked to the Southern Pacific system on 17 December 1887.

record of service with the Oregon Railway & Navigation Company. Villard's first move was to suggest to the Big Four in 1876 that they merge their California & Oregon with his Oregon Central (then Oregon & California). The Four were interested, but feigned disinterest, waiting for Villard's next move. Having achieved nothing, Villard began building south from Roseburg in 1881, nine years after Holladay halted construction. He reached Ashland, just short of the California border, in 1884. His railroad, exhausted and spent, went bankrupt the same year.

To the south, the Big Four had constructed no new California & Oregon tracks since the line had reached Redding in 1872. In 1887, three years after it failed, the Oregon & California finally joined the California & Oregon as part of the Southern Pacific system. Construction resumed immediately on the tracks across the Siskiyou Mountains north of Redding. They reached Ashland by year's end, and on 17 December 1887, Charles Crocker came north from San Francisco to drive the last spike of Southern Pacific's new Siskiyou line. The company thus had a continuous arc of steel linking Oregon, California, Arizona, New Mexico, Texas and Louisiana. A traveler could buy a ticket from a single company and travel from the mouth of the Columbia to the mouth of the Mississippi.

In 1888 Southern Pacific consolidated the railroad shops of two of its Texas subsidiaries, the GH&SA and the Texas & New Orleans Railroad. The resulting facility at Houston em-

---

## The Golden West: The Cotton Belt

**1877** The Tyler Tap Railroad, oldest part of the Cotton Belt, begins operations in Texas.

**1883** The Texas & St Louis Railway (the Cotton Belt) line between Bird's Point, Missouri, and Gatesville, Texas, is completed on 12 August at Rob Roy, Arkansas.

**1886** The Cotton Belt is converted from narrow to standard gauge.

**1888** The Cotton Belt reaches North Little Rock (Arkansas), Shreveport (Louisiana) and Fort Worth (Texas).

**1903** The Cotton Belt reaches St Louis in time for the 1904 World's Fair.

**1912** The Cotton Belt extends its lines across the Mississippi to Memphis, Tennessee.

**1932** The Southern Pacific gains 87 percent control of the Cotton Belt (known then as the St Louis Southwestern Railway Company).

**1972** The Interstate Commerce Commission permits the Cotton Belt to take over 50 percent control of the Alton & Southern.

**1980** Southern Pacific, in 98.34 percent control of the Cotton Belt (St Louis Southwestern Railway Company), adds a 992-mile extension to the Cotton Belt system. The extension (formerly part of the bankrupt Chicago, Rock Island & Pacific) extends from St Louis to Kansas City and southwest across Kansas and Oklahoma to Tucumcari, New Mexico.

---

ployed 5000 people and constituted the largest such facility in the entire Southwest, indicative of the enormous proportions to which the Southern Pacific had grown.

In the 20 years leading up to C P Huntington's 1890 ascendancy within Southern Pacific, the company had grown from a mere component of the first transcontinental line, with a nearly empty bank box, to an enormous network that dominated California and reached farther than any other railroad on the continent.

## The Cotton Belt

In 1883, the same year that Colonel Tom Pierce pounded the last spike of the Sunset Route into a tie west of the Pecos River, another historic spike was driven home several hundred miles to the northeast, at Rob Roy, Arkansas. The latter ceremony had its roots in the Tyler Tap Railroad, which began service in 1877 in northeastern Texas. A few years later, the Texas & St Louis Railway began operations through the cotton country of the lower Mississippi. This network of routes eventually formed the St Louis Southwestern Railroad, known as the Cotton Belt. Though the Cotton Belt did not become part of the Southern Pacific empire until 1932, it is worth noting the early development of the system for two reasons. First, Southern Pacific's Sunset Route had its terminus immediately to the south, and, second, the Cotton Belt was to become the largest Southern Pacific rail subsidiary.

On 12 August 1883, the silver spike driven at Rob Roy, Arkansas, connected the Cotton Belt's Texas operations (including the original Tyler Tap lines, which were the oldest tracks in the network) with the Cotton Belt lines running south along the Mississippi from Bird's Point, Missouri. Five years later, in 1888, the Cotton Belt extended its tracks into Little Rock, Shreveport and as far west as Fort Worth, Texas. It was not until 1903, however, that the Cotton Belt tracks were built to connect St Louis with the system.

# The Golden Years
# 1890-1917

**W**hen Collis P Huntington took over the Southern Pacific reins from Leland Stanford on 28 February 1890, the two decades of expansion that had defined the shape of the empire were over. With a few minor exceptions, the route map of 1890 was the same in 1980, and it spanned a distance greater than that of any other railroad in the United States. During the period from 1890 to 1917, this freshly assembled empire matured and developed, and its power burgeoned.

Within California, the company's power was so great that its offices in San Francisco had become the de facto capital of the state. Because it controlled California's transportation network, it was perceived as controlling the state itself. The phrase 'The Southern Pacific *is* the state of California' was coined. The state's people and her politicians lined up on either side of the issue of whether or not this power was wielded in the best interests of the state. While some saw the company as an important element of agricultural and in-dustrial development, others saw it only as a greedy monster, exploiting rather than developing California's resources. Some politicians ran on platforms built on the latter idea, and others were willing to support the Southern Pacific with or without remuneration. There is little doubt that the Big Four bought the services of judges and legislators during the final quarter of the nineteenth century, but this would not have happened were those services not for sale.

## Huntington at the Helm
Collis Huntington assumed Southern Pacific's presidency in 1890 after 29 years as vice-president and at least five years as the company's de facto president. He had spent most of those years in New York, where he made the deals and arranged

*Right:* **Engineer Jack Clark (left), fireman Tom Altridge (center) and machinist's helper Fred Jody (right), c1900.**

*Below: No 2127* **was built in 1888 and scrapped in 1933.**

Jack Clark
Engr.

Tom Abbit
Fireman

Fred Jody
Mach. Helper

the financing that kept the Southern Pacific afloat in its early days and made it vastly wealthy in later years. During that time his personal fortune did not suffer, either. In the year that he took over the company presidency, the *New York World* reckoned him to be the sixth wealthiest man in the United States, after John D Rockefeller, William Astor, Cornelius and William Vanderbilt, and his archrival Jay Gould.

Estimated at $40 million, the fortune Huntington controlled from his little office at 23 Broad Street included his interest not only in the Southern Pacific, but in a number of other endeavors as well. He had taken control of the Chesapeake & Ohio Railroad and several lesser railroads from Kentucky to Mexico. He owned the Newport News Shipbuilding Company at the mouth of Chesapeake Bay and the Pacific Mail Steamship Company that sailed from San Francisco Bay.

In 1890 only two of the Big Four remained, and with Stanford's semiretirement from Southern Pacific affairs, Huntington was in control. The company was doing well. Its virtual monopoly of freight traffic in much of the West, coupled with the expanding population and industry of the region, made the century's last decade a profitable one. In California, the Coast Line south of San Francisco was opened into San Luis Obispo in 1894. In 1898 Southern Pacific took control of the Sonora Railway in Mexico. The line ran from Nogales, Arizona, south to Guaymas on the Gulf of California, nearly 300 miles from the border, and it formed the basis for expansion a decade later.

## The Golden Years

**1890** The Sherman Antitrust Act is passed on 2 July, bringing the Southern Pacific-Central Pacific merger into question. C P Huntington assumes the Southern Pacific presidency from Leland Stanford.

**1891** Leland Stanford is elected to a second term as US senator from California.

**1892** C P Huntington's 900-mile Mexican International Railroad, begun in 1883, is completed from Eagle Pass, Texas, to Durango, Mexico.

**1893** Leland Stanford dies in Palo Alto on 21 June.

**1897** E H Harriman gains control of Union Pacific.

**1898** Southern Pacific buys control of the Sonora Railway from Benson, Arizona, to Guaymas, Mexico, via Nogales. A presidential commission is appointed to settle the Central Pacific debt and orders it to pay 20 semiannual payments. Southern Pacific's promotional magazine, *Sunset*, is founded.

**1899** On 16 February Southern Pacific agrees to take responsibility for the Central Pacific debt through stock purchases.

**1900** C P Huntington dies at Raquette Lake, New York, on 13 August.

**1901** E H Harriman, who controls 45 percent of Southern Pacific stock, assumes chairmanship of the executive committee in April and the presidency in September. Colonist fares are established to bring new settlers to California at budget rates. The Coast Line, from San Francisco to Los Angeles via Santa Barbara, is finally completed on 31 March.

**1902** The El Paso-to-Tucumcari, New Mexico, line is opened.

**1903** Southern Pacific takes 50 percent control of the Pacific Electric commuter railroad in Southern California (founded 1902).

*Top:* **Central Pacific *No 167* was built here at the Sacramento Shops in 1873. The roundhouse survived until 1927.**

*Above:* **C P Huntington, last of the Big Four.**

*Left:* **Southern Pacific employees in San Francisco in 1902.**

Collis Huntington, the last surviving member of the Four, died at Raquette Lake, New York, on 13 August 1900, having seen in a new century and succeeded during his final years in forestalling repayment of the Central Pacific's original federal construction loan. His fortune went to his widow and nephew (who eventually married one another), his fabulous art collection went to the Metropolitan Museum in New York, his effects went to the Huntington Library in Southern California and his presidency of the Southern Pacific went to Edward Henry Harriman.

## Edward Henry Harriman

The man who took control of the Southern Pacific a year after Huntington's death proved to be as competent a railroad man as he was a financier. Edward Henry Harriman had been buying and selling railroads since 1884, but had risen to prominence in 1897 when he took over the bankrupt Union Pacific and turned a profit in less than three years.

When Huntington died, he was temporarily succeeded as president by Charles Hays, but Harriman's eye was on the chair. Having just restored the Union Pacific to health, Harriman mortgaged it for $100 million and began buying Southern Pacific stock. A year after Huntington's death, he owned 45 percent of Southern Pacific and a month later, in September 1901, he assumed the presidency. Unlike many of the railroad barons of the era, who bought and sold railroads as though they were any other type of bauble, Harriman had a distinct interest in, and understanding of, railroading.

Harriman ordered an extensive refurbishment of the Southern Pacific. The improvements included straightening curves and rebuilding worn sections of track, such as the entire section of the transcontinental across Nevada that was replaced in 1902. The most spectacular bit of curve-

*Above:* **Edward H Harriman in 1909, the year of his death. He was president of Southern Pacific for eight years and aspired to a national railroad empire.**

*Below:* **Southern Pacific's *No 1307*, an 0-4-0 relic of the steam age.**

# Southern Pacific Company--Pacific System

## COAST DIVISION

# SPECIAL TIME TABLE

— FOR THE —

## "PRESIDENT'S SPECIAL"

To take effect Friday, May 10, 1901, at 2 o'clock, P. M., and void after 10 P. M., Tuesday, May 14, 1901

The "President's Special" will leave Santa Barbara May 10, 1901, and run to San Francisco on the following time, and will have absolute right of track over all trains, which must clear its time thirty minutes:

| Friday, May 10 | | |
|---|---|---|
| Leave Santa Barbara.... | 2.00 p. m. | |
| " Irma ........... | 2.08 | " |
| " Goleta........... | 2.16 | " |
| " La Patera....... | 2.19 | " |
| " Coromar ........ | 2.23 | " |
| " Elwood .......... | 2.26 | " |
| " Naples .......... | 2.36 | " |
| " Capitan ......... | 2.49 | " |
| " Orella .......... | 2.53 | " |
| " Tajiguas ........ | 3.00 | " |
| " Gaviota.......... | 3.16 | " |
| " Sacate ......... | 3.29 | " |
| " Santa Anita...... | 3.30 | " |
| " San Augustin .... | 3.38 | " |
| " Gato ........... | 3.41 | " |
| " Concepcion ...... | 3.53 | " |
| " Jalama .......... | 4.05 | " |
| " Leda ........... | 4.09 | " |
| " Sudden ......... | 4.14 | " |
| " Arguello........ | 4.25 | " |
| " Honda .......... | 4.38 | " |
| " Surf .......... | 4.51 | " |
| " Tangair .... ... | 5.06 | " |
| " Narlon ......... | 5.15 | " |
| " Antonio ......... | 5.24 | " |
| " Casmalia........ | 5.30 | " |
| " Schumann ....... | 5.37 | " |
| " Waldorf ........ | 5.47 | " |
| " Guadalupe ...... | 5.58 | " |
| " Bromela ........ | 6.08 | " |
| " Callender ....... | 6.15 | " |
| " Oceano ......... | 6.25 | " |
| " Grover ...... ... | 6.30 | " |
| " Edna ........ | 6.45 | " |
| Arrive San Luis Obispo.. | 7.00 | " |
| Leave San Luis Obispo.. | 8.00 | " |
| " Ramona Hotel.... | 8.02 | " |

| | | |
|---|---|---|
| Leave Hathaway Ave... | 8.03 p. m. | |
| " Goldtree ........ | 8.11 | " |
| " Serrano.......... | 8.24 | " |
| " Cuesta.......... | 8.36 | " |
| " Santa Margarita.. | 8.45 | " |
| " Havel .......... | 8.55 | " |
| " Atascadero....... | 9.00 | " |
| " Asuncion ........ | 9.07 | " |
| " Templeton ....... | 9.14 | " |
| " Paso Robles ...... | 9.25 | " |
| " Wellsona ....... | 9.36 | " |
| " San Miguel ...... | 9.44 | " |
| " Nacimiento ...... | 9.56 | " |
| " Bradley.......... | 10.07 | " |
| " Wunpost ....... | 10.20 | " |
| " San Ardo ....... | 10.35 | " |
| " Upland ........ | 10.45 | " |
| " San Lucas........ | 10.56 | " |
| " Welby.......... | 11.06 | " |
| " Kings City...... | 11.14 | " |
| " Coburn ......... | 11.24 | " |
| " Metz ...:...... | 11.37 | " |
| " Riverbank ....... | 11.47 | " |
| " Soledad.......... | 11.56 | " |
| " Camphora.May 11. | 12.01 | a. m. |
| " Gonzales........ | 12.12 | " |
| " Chualar ........ | 12.24 | " |
| " Spence ......... | 12.32 | " |
| " Spreckels Junc... | 12.40 | " |
| " Salinas ......... | 12.45 | " |
| " Graves ......... | 12.49 | " |
| " Cooper ....... | 12 52 | " |
| " Castroville ...... | 1.00 | " |
| " Morocojo ........ | 1.08 | " |
| " Neponset ........ | 1.11 | " |
| " Bardin .......... | 1.20 | " |
| " Seaside ........ | 1.54 | " |
| Arrive Del Monte ...... | 2.00 | " |

(OVER)

*Above:* **Presidents William McKinley and Theodore Roosevelt were among the earliest US presidents to visit California on official business, and Southern Pacific provided the special trains that carried them on their tours throughout the state.**

**Posing beside locomotive *No 1453*, President Roosevelt's personal train, are (left to right) Dan Kellogg, assistant master mechanic; Bob Aiken, engineer; Jack Muhr, boilermaker clerk; Fred Sugden, fireman, and Harry Stevenson, road foreman of engines. President McKinley's train, locomotive *No 8*, is shown steaming into Oakland in May 1901. The timetable for this visit appears at the left.**

*Left:* Snow was as much of an obstacle in keeping the railroad open as it had been in building it. This Southern Pacific snowplow train carried extra gangs to Cascade, in the high Sierra, during the disastrous winter of 1889-90 to clear snow off the main line. The railroad employed more than 4000 shovelers and another 500 men to sledge supplies and feed the army of workers. The winter of 1866-67, when more than 40 feet of snow fell, had severely hampered construction of the tracks over the Sierra.

straightening undertaken during this era was the construction of the Lucin Cutoff, a 16-mile rock-filled causeway and 12-mile wooden trestle across the northern end of Great Salt Lake. When the original tracks were laid in 1869, the company was in a race with the Union Pacific and had detoured around the northern perimeter of the lake. The Lucin Cutoff, completed in 1903, reduced the distance from California to Ogden by 44 miles. Ironically, the section north of the lake, which was then just a siding, included Promontory, the site of the original golden spike ceremony. Thus the site that had seen the historic meeting of the Central Pacific and the Union Pacific was deleted from the main line.

## Disaster on the Colorado

The huge Colorado River, which cuts the Grand Canyon, flows westward out of the canyon and then south, forming the border between Arizona and California. On the California side lies the Imperial Valley, which was turned into an area of rich farmland by means of irrigation water from the Colorado. The lowest point of the Imperial Valley, once the Salton Sink, is 287 feet below sea level and hence somewhat farther below the river's level. In July 1905, after a winter of heavy snows in the Rockies where the Colorado originates, the river began to overflow. The rampaging waters threatened to flood the

*Below:* Southern Pacific's *Overland Limited* steams over the famous Lucin Cutoff across Great Salt Lake in Utah. Nearly 13 miles of the 32-mile cutoff were built on a trestle consisting of about 27,000 piles. Erected at a cost of $8,400,000, this cutoff was the greatest construction project on the original transcontinental railroad since the herculean task of building the western link was completed in 1869.

whole corner of the state and turn the Imperial Valley into a lake. The Southern Pacific took on the job of trying to contain the flood, and had to rebuild its own tracks several times as the waters rose. The Southern Pacific tracks through the sink eventually ended up under 74 feet of water, and the Salton Sink became the Salton Sea. The disruption affected 1200 miles of Southern Pacific lines.

Because part of the break lay in Mexico, and because the US Government was not in a position to act quickly, President Theodore Roosevelt asked Harriman and the Southern Pacific to save the Imperial Valley. Roosevelt generously promised to reimburse the railroad for the cost of the operation. Harriman ordered all the railroad's resources into the effort. Track was laid across temporary bridges built over the breaks in the river's shoreline. Boulders as large as 15 tons were then hauled in to be dumped into the breaks in an attempt to close them. On 11 February 1907, the work was over. Southern Pacific had succeeded. The enormous task had seen huge volumes of rock moved faster than ever before in history, but the cost had been an equally enormous $4 million. The bill was presented to the US Government for the promised payment. When it was finally settled 23 years later, the government paid the railroad only 25 cents for each dollar it had spent.

## The Government Versus the Railroad
The disagreement between the federal government and the Southern Pacific Company over payment of expenses incurred during the rescue of the Imperial Valley was only one item on a list of financial disagreements between the two entities. Most of these disagreements fell into one of two categories. The first was repayment of the original loans to Central Pacific for the construction of the transcontinental under the Railroad Act of 1862, and the second was federal government antitrust actions.

In the first category, President Grover Cleveland initiated an investigation in 1887 that showed that the Central Pacific component by itself could not repay the debt, and that the Southern Pacific component had not diverted any business from Central Pacific to keep that component artificially poor. Three years later, on 17 February 1890, the same month that Huntington took over as president, a US Senate committee recommended that the Southern Pacific Company be compelled to pay the Central Pacific debt. Nine years less one day later, on 16 February 1899, Huntington finally agreed that Southern Pacific would gradually pay off the debt in a series of 20 semiannual payments by buying bonds totaling $125 million from Central Pacific. On 1 February 1909 the final installment of the $58,813,000 was paid in full.

The government's antitrust actions followed a course somewhat contradictory to its debt-recovery activities. On 2 July 1890, a month before Huntington died, the Sherman Antitrust Act went into effect. Under its provisions, the merger of the Central Pacific and the Southern Pacific was liable to dissolution as an unfair monopoly. While one hand of the government held that the two lines should be broken up, the other hand held that they should remain together to pay the Central Pacific's debt. It was not until 11 February 1914, five years after the final payment of the Central Pacific debt, that the government, as threatened, filed suit to compel Southern Pacific to sell its control of Central Pacific. The matter was not finally settled until 6 February 1923, when the Interstate Commerce Commission (ICC) ruled that the ownership of both the Southern Pacific Railroad and the Central Pacific

The Southern Pacific right of way was submerged in water when the Colorado River overflowed into the Salton Sink in 1905. It took two years to return the river to its channel to save the Imperial Valley.

Railroad by the Southern Pacific Company was in the public interest.

Although the Southern Pacific and the Central Pacific had merged operationally in 1870 and officially in 1885, Harriman maintained his Union Pacific and Southern Pacific holdings as generally separate operating entities. Six years prior to its action against the Southern Pacific/Central Pacific trust, the US Government brought suit against Harriman for owning and operating both the Union Pacific and Southern Pacific. The suit was brought on 1 February 1908, almost a year to the week after the Southern Pacific saved the Imperial Valley. Harriman fought the government on this issue for the last 19 years of his life. After his death in September 1909, the battle finally went all the way to the US Supreme Court, which issued a decision compelling the Harriman flagship, Union Pacific, to relinquish control of the Southern Pacific Company. The net result of the federal government's intervention in railroad affairs was an end to 12 years of marriage between Union Pacific and the Southern Pacific Company. Another result was legal vindication of the Southern Pacific Company's longstanding ownership of both the Central Pacific and the Southern Pacific railroads.

## Triumph Over Disaster

The legal troubles bedeviling the Southern Pacific Company were not the only adversity that it had to face during the century's first decade. On 18 April 1906, San Francisco, the hub of the empire, was struck by one of the worst earthquakes in recorded history. The company's offices were built on the soft ground near sea level and collapsed into a pile of dusty bricks. The grand mansions of the Big Four atop the rocky mass of Nob Hill survived the quake, but were destroyed within days by the devastating fire that followed the earthquake and gutted much of the city. Though trains had been derailed and tracks damaged, Southern Pacific crews went into action, evacuating 224,000 people from the affected area and rushing relief supplies.

# The Golden Years

**1904** The Lucin Cutoff built across Great Salt Lake opens for service on 8 March, bypassing Promontory. Tracks of the Coast Line, opened in 1901, are actually finished along the California coast between Santa Barbara and Los Angeles on 20 March.

**1905** A series of floods on the Colorado River threaten to inundate California's Imperial Valley. Southern Pacific undertakes to return the river to its channel.

**1906** San Francisco suffers an 8.3 earthquake on 18 April. Southern Pacific's offices and the Nob Hill mansions of the now-deceased Big Four are destroyed in the subsequent fire. President Roosevelt asks Harriman to help save the Imperial Valley at government expense. The Pacific Fruit Express (PFE) is established as a joint venture of Southern Pacific and Union Pacific.

**1907** The Northwestern Pacific Railroad, a consolidation of seven small lines on California's north coast, come under joint Southern Pacific/AT&SF control on 8 January. Southern Pacific closes the Colorado River break on 11 February. The Bayshore Cutoff south of San Francisco is completed.

**1908** The Rocklin, California, terminal is moved to Roseville.

**1909** The last of Central Pacific's government debt, plus interest, is finally paid off. Southern Pacific de Mexico is formed to build a rail line from Guaymas to Guadalajara. E H Harriman dies on 9 September.

**1910** Mallet cab-ahead locomotives are put into service with Southern Pacific. The Pecos River Bridge is strengthened by doubling its weight in steel.

**1911** William Sproule becomes Southern Pacific president on 25 September.

**1913** Southern Pacific is now operating 1400 trains daily. The Supreme Court decides that Union Pacific must sell all of its Southern Pacific stock.

**1914** The government begins its suit on 11 February to compel Southern Pacific to sell its Central Pacific stock (the issue is resolved in 1923).

**1915** The Panama Pacific Exposition in San Francisco results in a 65 percent boost in Southern Pacific passenger traffic. New stations open in San Francisco and Los Angeles. Northwestern Pacific opens the Eureka Line through the Eel River Canyon on 1 July. Pacific Mail Steamship service is discontinued.

*Left:* **An emergency lunchroom was set up at the San Francisco Ferry Building after the earthquake and fire of 1906. E H Harriman is seated at the left.**

*Below:* **The *Overland Limited* pulls into Oakland in 1908. The American battleship fleet arrived in San Francisco on 8 May, and the USS *Iowa* can be seen in the background.**

*Below:* Resource-rich California supplies the rest of the nation with its great bounty of agricultural products. This trainload of wine from the Chateau Martin Winery is headed for markets in New York.

*Bottom:* Southern Pacific assumed ownership of railroad lines in California's redwood country through its subsidiary Northwestern Pacific. This shipment was destined for San Francisco, where the lumber was used to build the city.

*Right:* Flame Tokay grapes are ready to be loaded on trains in Sacramento for shipment to distant markets. California produces 85 percent of the nation's grapes.

Despite the dual disaster, the company not only rebuilt the San Francisco facilities, but went ahead with other planned improvements and expansions. From temporary general offices on Market Street, it began work in 1906 on Harriman's plan to run a double set of tracks over the Sierra. In 1907 Southern Pacific joined with the rival Atchison, Topeka & Santa Fe Railroad in a venture known as the Northwestern Pacific Railroad Company. This was a consolidation of seven small companies like the North Pacific Coast Railroad that had been operating in the redwood forests of California's coast north of San Francisco. By 1913 Southern Pacific was operating 1400 trains a day. Two years later, with the start of the Panama-Pacific Exposition in San Francisco, passenger traffic into the new Southern Pacific terminal at Third and Townsend grew by 65 percent.

## Agricultural Development

Southern Pacific's efforts to attract settlers to California's potential farmland, which began in the 1870s with completion of the transcontinental, by no means declined under the stewardship of Huntington and Harriman. The company continued to sell its land-grant acreage to small farmers and set up financing programs to help them buy it. In 1889 the Southern Pacific Colonization Agency was established and oriented toward attracting smaller farmers to the state. Between 1870 and 1900, California's population grew by 265 percent with many, if not most, of the new settlers coming west on the company's rails.

In the 1880s the Southern Pacific initiated 'colonist fares,' which brought people to California from Chicago for $33 and from Missouri River points for $25. The colonist fares are estimated to have brought 800,000 new settlers into the state.

As settlers streamed westward aboard the company's trains, the eastbound trains carried the state's agricultural products to a hungry nation. The Southern Pacific not only shipped the fruits of California's fields and vineyards, but went out of its way to help farmers promote their produce. Professor Richard Orsi, writing in the *California Historial Quarterly,* notes that when agricultural 'co-operatives finally emerged in the 1880s and 1890s, the railroad assisted them by encouraging farmers to join, improving refrigeration technology, running express fruit trains, and sponsoring advertising campaigns to widen and organize California fruit markets. Beginning with the Centennial Exposition of 1876, the Southern Pacific sent costly displays to Eastern fairs, which helped establish California's reputation as a leading fruit-growing region. As the company matured, it developed more specialized and systematic advertising techniques. In 1907 the Southern Pacific offered to match the advertising budget of the California Fruit Growers' Exchange in a concerted effort to expand Eastern consumption of California oranges.

'From 1907 to 1911, the railroad and the Exchange co-operated to send lecturers, displays, posters and *California Fruit Special* trains to the Middle West and other areas to increase orange sales severalfold, to establish the Sunkist brand name, and, incidentally, to stimulate migration to

**Southern Pacific's wood and plaster pavilion for the 1915 Panama-Pacific Exposition was torn down after the fair.**

California. Smaller-scale campaigns after 1900 also assisted the organized growers of raisins, prunes and other deciduous fruits. Frequently, railroad propaganda aimed at changing the eating habits of the young. The *California Prune Primer*, a 1901 pamphlet designed as a supplemental reader for elementary school children and sent by the company to 100,000 teachers across the country, created a mild sensation. Teachers and parents deluged the railroad with requests for extra copies. Within a few months more than 500,000 had been distributed. The outcome of this experiment led the company to issue other California primers with equal success.'

In 1898 the Southern Pacific began publication of its monthly promotional magazine, *Sunset*. The magazine carried articles promoting the West to outsiders and promulgating new agricultural ideas and procedures to Westerners.

In 1914 *Sunset* was sold to a private publisher, and it is still appearing more than 70 years later. From its offices at 576 Sacramento Street in San Francisco, *Sunset* communicated the message of California's rich land, mild climate and easy lifestyle to the rest of the nation.

Southern Pacific developed insulated boxcars that could be turned into rolling refrigerators by adding block ice through ports in the top. These refrigerator cars, or 'reefers' as they were better known, became the basis for the Pacific Fruit Express (PFE), formed jointly by Southern Pacific and Union Pacific in 1906. The distinctive yellow cars of the PFE traveled across the nation, carrying the lettuce, oranges, table grapes and apples of the Pacific states to consumers in distant markets who had formerly gone without many fresh fruits and vegetables during the winter months. The two companies continued joint ownership of PFE until 1977, when it became a separate entity as a Southern Pacific subsidiary.

## Consolidation

The years between 1900 and 1917 saw tremendous growth in the West. The infrastructure laid down by the Southern Pacific and other railroads in the preceding years provided a framework for both agricultural and industrial development. Despite the services it performed and the public support it received, the Southern Pacific became a favorite target of zealous crusaders and issue-hungry politicians. Hiram Johnson was elected governor of California in 1910 on a platform of driving the company out of state politics. The federal government had asked the Southern Pacific to save the Imperial Valley, and when the task was accomplished, it responded to trying to break up the company. Ultimately, the company survived these adversities while bringing taxpayers into the western states and generating the jobs that sparked true economic growth. New tracks were laid on old routes, and additional routes enlarged the existing network. New lines were added to the system both north and south of San Francisco.

Edward Henry Harriman died on 9 September 1909 and was succeeded as president by Robert Lovett, who served for two years until he was replaced by William Sproule in 1911. The company's general offices, destroyed in the 1906 earthquake, were re-established on Market Street near Powell, where they remained pending completion of the new Southern Pacific building at the foot of Market Street overlooking the Ferry Building and San Francisco Bay.

# The Golden Century
## 1917-1985

ompletion of the huge red-brick Southern Pacific
Building at 65 Market Street in San Francisco in 1917
marked the beginning of a new era in the company's
history. The age of the pioneers was gone, as were all the
great nineteenth-century industrialists who had built the
largest spread of railroad trackage in the United States. The
business at hand had turned from building an empire to
running a railroad. The Southern Pacific had entered the
twentieth century.

The grand opening of the new symbol of Southern
Pacific's power took place against the backdrop of the
twentieth century's first great war, the first major conflict to
affect the United States since the Civil War more than half a
century earlier. The United States entered World War I in
April, and the Southern Pacific was called upon to increase its
capacity dramatically almost overnight. The nation's entire
rail network was soon doing double duty, transporting men
and supplies to embarkation points on the East and Gulf
coasts. The problem of integrating the dozens of railroads in
the United States proved insurmountable for the federal
government. Washington decided that it was the best-
equipped entity to manage the war effort of the American
railroad system, and on 28 December 1917, the railroads

were nationalized. For 26 months thereafter, until 1 March
1920, the Southern Pacific was a government employee.
Both the government and the railroads learned from the
experience – and from the enormous, frustrating rail traffic
jams that ensued through 1918. The railroads saw the need
for more sidings and larger yards to cope with such an
emergency, and the government learned that railroads are
best run by railroad companies.

## The Roaring Twenties
The decade that followed the return of the railroads to private
ownership was an era of expansion for the entire American
economy, particularly that of the West, where California's
population grew by 65 percent. For the Southern Pacific,
profits grew steadily. In 1922 the 'Prosperity Special,' a train
consisting of 20 brand-new Baldwin locomotives, crossed the
country to join the Southern Pacific's growing fleet.

*Right:* **Construction of the new offices began in 1916. The
view below shows progress after three months, and *above* in
April 1917, five months before completion.**

*Below: No 2488* **is typical of the Pacific 4-6-2s ordered in
1904 for heavy passenger trains on slightly graded routes.**

## The Golden Century

**1917** Southern Pacific moves into its new General Office Building at 65 Market Street in San Francisco in July. The federal government takes over control of American railroads on 28 December for 26 months because of World War I.

**1919** The San Diego & Arizona Railway subsidiary (later San Diego & Arizona Eastern) is completed to El Centro in the Imperial Valley.

**1922** The 'Prosperity Special,' 20 new Baldwin locomotives, cross the continent to be put into service with the Southern Pacific. Forerunners of the *Daylights* make their first San Francisco-to-Los Angeles runs.

**1923** The Interstate Commerce Commission finally decides that Southern Pacific's control of the Central Pacific is in the public interest.

**1924** The El Paso & Southwestern Railroad is acquired by Southern Pacific on 1 November, adding new track from Tucson to Tucumcari by way of El Paso.

**1925** The double tracking of the Sierra route, including a 10,326-foot tunnel, is completed.

**1926** The 270-mile Cascade Line is opened for freight and local traffic on 1 September. The second Arizona main line (via Phoenix) is opened on 14 November. Southern Pacific purchases the Nevada California Oregon Railway, which will be put into service in 1929 as the Modoc Line.

**1927** The Southern Pacific de Mexico line to Guadalajara (1370 miles) opens on 17 April. Southern Pacific Motor Transport begins bus service in Oregon.

**1929** Pacific Motor Trucking Company, the Southern Pacific trucking subsidiary, begins service. The Modoc Line, acquired in 1926, is opened for service after having been converted from narrow to standard gauge.

*Left:* **Samuel Vauclain beside the 'Prosperity Special' of 2-10-2s that left the Baldwin Locomotive Works in July 1922.**

*Below:* **A second Sunset Route main line was added through Phoenix in 1926 *(left)*. Tucson *(right)* was always on the line.**

*Above:* **The railroad bridge over Suisun Bay was the largest and heaviest west of the Mississippi when finished in 1930.**

*Left:* **Baggage clerks at work at Houston Station in Texas.**

*Above right:* **Passengers pause at the Yuma, Arizona, station to sample the wares of a local artisan.**

The El Paso & Southwestern Railroad became part of Southern Pacific on 1 November 1924, and by 1925 the double tracks over the Sierra were completed. On 14 November 1926, a new main line through Phoenix, north of the original Sunset Route, was opened. During the 1920s, Southern Pacific more than doubled its empire in northern California and southern Oregon. The new 270-mile Cascade Line, paralleling the Siskiyou Line, was opened to freight traffic on 1 September 1926 and to through-passenger traffic on 17 April 1927. The narrow-gauge Nevada California Oregon Railway was purchased in 1926 and retracked with standard gauge in three years. In 1929 it reopened as Southern Pacific's Modoc Line, serving three states and reaching as far north as Klamath Falls, Oregon. The company now had three major north-south lines between central California and southern Oregon – the Cascade, the Siskiyou and the Modoc.

Serving the rugged hills of California's north coast was the Northwestern Pacific Railroad, which had been jointly owned by the Southern Pacific and the Sante Fe since 1907. In 1929 Southern Pacific took complete control of the 515-mile system and integrated its San Francisco Bay ferryboats into the Southern Pacific ferry system. While some ferry lines were being added, others were being taken out of service. The Big Four had acquired the California Pacific Railroad in 1876,

giving them a rail line from Sacramento to Benicia on Suisun Bay near the mouth of the Sacramento River, as well as a ferry line from Benicia to Oakland. In 1929 Southern Pacific began work on a bridge to span Suisun Bay, connecting Benicia on the north side with Martinez on the south. The resulting double-track bridge was 5603 feet long and the heaviest railroad bridge west of the Mississippi when it opened on 15 October 1930. One of the major Southern Pacific construction projects of the decade, it cost $10 million but provided direct rail service between Sacramento and Oakland by the shortest possible route.

During the prosperous 1920s, automobiles and trucks proliferated. Truck registrations tripled during the decade, and in California trucking grew at twice the national average. In response to what might have proven to be competition to its freight service, the Southern Pacific started the Pacific Motor Trucking Company (PMT) in 1929. The PMT was a coordinated truck/train freight system that permitted Southern Pacific to offer both the volume of railcars and the flexibility of trucks. In the meantime, the Southern Pacific responded to the need for low-density passenger service in Oregon, and in 1927 established its own bus line (later sold to Greyhound) called the Southern Pacific Motor Transport Company.

## Southern Pacific de Mexico

As early as the 1870s, CP Huntington had had interests in railroads south of the border. He had a controlling interest in the Mexican International Railroad (between Eagle Pass, Texas, and Durango, Mexico) and owned the title to another, unbuilt, railroad in Guatemala. It was 1898, however, before the Southern Pacific extended its operations below the

border of the United States. In that year the company took control of the Sonora Railway, which ran due south to Guaymas from Nogales on the Arizona/Mexico border. The Sonora Railway also owned a bit of track in Arizona that connected Nogales with Benson on the main line of Southern Pacific's Sunset Route.

It was decided to extend the line south from Guaymas to Guadalajara, near Mexico City; in 1905 construction began moving south from Empalme Junction near Guaymas, then north from Mazatlan in 1907. The Southern Pacific Railroad Company of Mexico (Southern Pacific de Mexico) was formed in 1909 to operate the line, which by 1913 was open from Nogales to Tepic. The remaining 102 miles into Guadalajara, however, remained unfinished until 1927. The territory involved was a washboard of razorback ridges and volcanic escarpments. It proved to be some of the hardest railroad construction in transportation history, necessitating the drilling of 32 tunnels. In addition to the natural obstacles, there was the problem of political unrest. Mexico was shaken by revolution. Anarchy reigned in many parts of the country, and the Yaqui Indians went on the warpath. Not only was construction halted, but a 105-mile section of Southern Pacific de Mexico track immediately north of Tepic could be operated for only five months between 1910 and 1920.

The costly project was finally completed in 1927, with a Southern Pacific network totaling 1370 miles and extending to Guadalajara where, as planned, it linked up with the Mexican National Railway line from Mexico City. The Southern Pacific de Mexico subsidiary was operated, at a loss, until 1951, when it was finally sold to the Mexican Government.

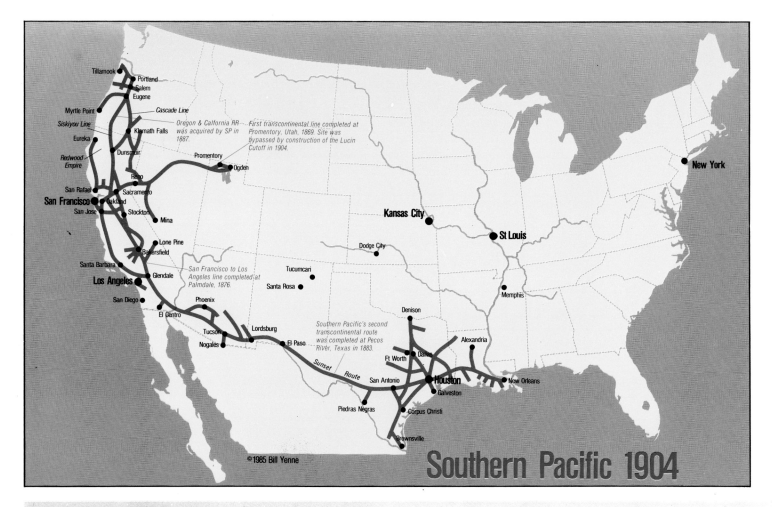

Tillamook
Portland
Salem
Eugene

*Cascade Line*

Myrtle Point

*Siskiyou Line*

Eureka

*Redwood Empire*

Klamath Falls

Dunsmuir

Promentory

*Oregon & Calfornia RR was acquired by SP in 1887.*

*First transcontinental line completed at Promentory, Utah, 1869. Site was bypassed by construction of the Lucin Cutoff in 1904.*

Reno

Ogden

San Rafael
Sacramento
**San Francisco**
Oakland
San Jose
Stockton
Mina

Lone Pine

Santa Barbara
Bakersfield

**Los Angeles**
Glendale

San Diego

El Centro

Phoenix

Tucson

Nogales

Lordsburg

El Paso

*San Francisco to Los Angeles line completed at Palmdale, 1876.*

Santa Rosa

Tucumcari

Dodge City

**Kansas City**

**St Louis**

Memphis

**New York**

*Southern Pacific's second transcontinental route was completed at Pecos River, Texas in 1883.*

*Sunset Route*

Denison

Ft Worth
Dallas

San Antonio

**Houston**
Galveston

Alexandria

New Orleans

Piedras Negras

Corpus Christi

Brownsville

©1985 Bill Yenne

## Southern Pacific 1904

**No 5000, with a 4-10-2 wheel configuration, was typical of those locomotives in service throughout Southern Pacific's vast network during the 1930s.**

SOUTHERN PACIFIC LINES

5000

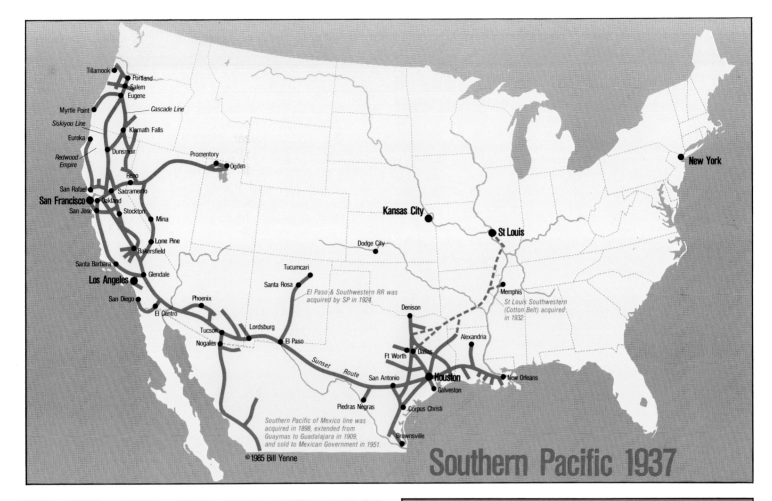

Tillamook
Portland
Salem
Eugene
Myrtle Point
*Cascade Line*
*Siskiyou Line*
Klamath Falls
Eureka
Dunsmuir
Promentory
Ogden
Reno
San Rafael
Sacramento
San Francisco
Oakland
San Jose
Stockton
Mina
Lone Pine
Santa Barbara
Glendale
Los Angeles
San Diego
Phoenix
El Centro
Tucson
Lordsburg
Nogales
El Paso
Santa Rosa
Tucumcari

*El Paso & Southwestern RR was acquired by SP in 1924*

Dodge City
Kansas City
St Louis
Memphis

*St Louis Southwestern (Cotton Belt) acquired in 1932*

New York

Denison
Alexandria
Ft Worth
Dallas
Houston
New Orleans
San Antonio
Galveston
Piedras Negras
Corpus Christi
Brownsville

*Sunset Route*

*Southern Pacific of Mexico line was acquired in 1898, extended from Guaymas to Guadalajara in 1909, and sold to Mexican Government in 1951.*

©1985 Bill Yenne

## Southern Pacific 1937

## The Golden Century

**1930** The $10 million double-track bridge over the Suisun Bay, 35 miles north of San Francisco, is opened. Coordinated train/truck overnight delivery service is initiated. The peak year for Southern Pacific ferry service on San Francisco Bay sees 43 boats carry 40 million passengers and 6 million automobiles. The first centralized traffic control is established in April on 40 miles of track between Stockton and Sacramento.

**1931** Automatic block signals are completed on all Southern Pacific main lines.

**1932** Southern Pacific acquires control of the Cotton Belt with 87 percent ownership on 14 April. Southern Pacific posts record losses as the Great Depression bottoms out. Angus McDonald assumes the Southern Pacific presidency.

**1934** On 30 June the 12 lines composing Southern Pacific operations in Texas and Louisiana are consolidated under Southern Pacific's Texas & New Orleans Railroad.

**1935** The *Overnights,* fast merchandise freight trains, are introduced. A new government-built railroad bridge opens across the Mississippi at New Orleans. A system is introduced for teletyping waybills.

**1936** Business improves and new rolling stock is acquired as the Depression wanes. The first streamliner in the West, the *City of San Francisco,* begins service between Ogden and San Francisco. The San Francisco-Oakland Bay Bridge, the first of the bridges across San Francisco Bay is completed, spelling doom for Southern Pacific's ferryboat system.

**1937** The *Daylight* streamliners enter service between San Francisco and Los Angeles. The *Sunbeam* streamliners enter service between Dallas and Houston. Electromagnetic brakes are first used on Southern Pacific trains. Southern Pacific's Sacramento Shops build their last steam locomotive, having built over 200 since 1872.

## Crash and Depression

The 1920s had been good for Southern Pacific. Net profits had increased 55 percent, from $31.2 million in 1922 to an all-time high of $48.4 million in 1929. With the sudden onset of the Depression, net profits plummeted to $29.8 million in 1930 and to $3.9 million in 1931, just 8 percent of the 1929 net. The following year, 1932, was the lowest point of the Depression. Southern Pacific lost money for the first time in its history and missed a dividend for the first time since 1905, the year of the Imperial Valley flood. The railroad's revenue ton-miles had dropped by half since 1929 – the greatest decline in company history. The $9.5-million loss in 1932 was followed by a $9.3-million loss in 1933. It was 1936 before the company managed to struggle out of the red ink to turn a profit of $11.2 million.

It was in the darkest hour, 1932, that Angus David McDonald came to the helm of Southern Pacific. A quiet, unsmiling, former football player from Notre Dame who had joined the company in 1901, McDonald walked daily from his Nob Hill home down to the company's headquarters at the foot of Market Street. There he faced the difficult decisions and made the difficult cuts in maintenance and manpower that ultimately saved the company.

## Recovery

As Angus McDonald pulled the company out of the Depression, it regained the vitality of its halcyon days. Profits were low at first, but they were growing again, and growing at a healthy rate. The cuts that McDonald had been forced to make in 1932 had been deep, but most of the company's muscle was intact. As the Depression waned in late 1937, the company was in an enviable position.

Southern Pacific was the third biggest industrial corporation in the United States, exceeded only by AT&T and the then gargantuan Pennsylvania Railroad. The San Francisco-

*Above:* **Southern Pacific officials at Los Angeles in 1922. From left, William Sproule, Julius Kruttschnit, Angus McDonald and Paul Shoup. Sproule was the current company president. Kruttschnitt, chairman since 1913, had been president as well between 1918 and 1920. McDonald was the controller and assumed the presidency 10 years later. Shoup was president between 1929 and 1932. (See table on page 127.)**

*Below: No 5009 was a late-model steam engine.*

based corporation exceeded in size such giants as General Motors, US Steel, all of the Standard Oil companies and the New York Central Railroad. Its 16,000 miles of track spread farther and wider than those of any other railroad in the United States. By virtue of owning the Morgan Steamship Line out of New Orleans, Southern Pacific was the nation's only coast-to-coast system.

In terms of passenger revenue, the company was by far the West's largest railroad in 1937, and was nearly tied for third place nationally. Passenger revenues for the five top US railroad companies were as follows:

1. Pennsylvania Railroad                  $67,652,000
2. New York Central Railroad             $63,300,000
3. New York, New Haven & Hartford        $24,990,000
4. Southern Pacific Company              $24,578,000
5. Atchison, Topeka & Santa Fe           $15,630,000

Passenger revenue, however, accounted for only 12 percent of the company's revenues. Freight was king. Southern Pacific carried 65 percent of the nation's copper ore, 33 percent of its watermelons and 22 percent of its logs. By 1937 the company operated 36,646 refrigerator cars, which were monitored by telegraph so that they could be diverted en route if the owner of their contents found a better market for his produce.

The year 1937 was a turning point in other ways as well. It was the year that the last steam locomotive was built at the Sacramento Shops, and that the glamorous streamliners were introduced. Their names, *Californian, Forty Niner, Cascade, Challenger, Sunbeam* and most famous of all, *Daylight,* have

**Right:** Angus D McDonald guided Southern Pacific through the Depression and kept it from going into bankruptcy. It was the only major US railroad never to be in receivership.

**Below:** The dining room at Houston Station in 1934.

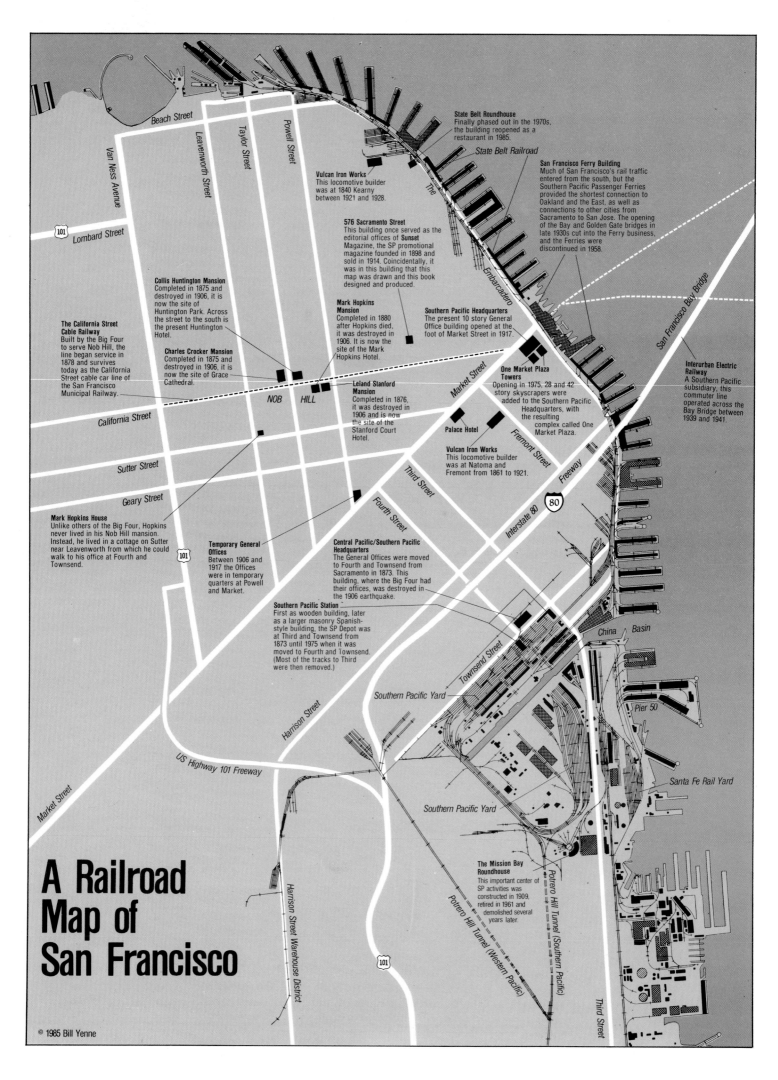

**Beach Street**

**Van Ness Avenue**

**Leavenworth Street**

**Taylor Street**

**Powell Street**

**101** **Lombard Street**

**State Belt Roundhouse**
Finally phased out in the 1970s, the building reopened as a restaurant in 1985.

**State Belt Railroad**

**Vulcan Iron Works**
This locomotive builder was at 1840 Kearny between 1921 and 1928.

**San Francisco Ferry Building**
Much of San Francisco's rail traffic entered from the south, but the Southern Pacific Passenger Ferries provided the shortest connection to Oakland and the East, as well as connections to other cities from Sacramento to San Jose. The opening of the Bay and Golden Gate bridges in late 1930s cut into the Ferry business, and the Ferries were discontinued in 1958.

**576 Sacramento Street**
This building once served as the editorial offices of **Sunset** Magazine, the SP promotional magazine founded in 1898 and sold in 1914. Coincidentally, it was in this building that this map was drawn and this book designed and produced.

**Collis Huntington Mansion**
Completed in 1875 and destroyed in 1906, it is now the site of Huntington Park. Across the street to the south is the present Huntington Hotel.

**Mark Hopkins Mansion**
Completed in 1880 after Hopkins died, it was destroyed in 1906. It is now the site of the Mark Hopkins Hotel.

**Southern Pacific Headquarters**
The present 10 story General Office building opened at the foot of Market Street in 1917.

**The California Street Cable Railway**
Built by the Big Four to serve Nob Hill, the line began service in 1878 and survives today as the California Street cable car line of the San Francisco Municipal Railway.

**Charles Crocker Mansion**
Completed in 1875 and destroyed in 1906, it is now the site of Grace Cathedral.

**Leland Stanford Mansion**
Completed in 1876, it was destroyed in 1906 and is now the site of the Stanford Court Hotel.

**NOB HILL**

**One Market Plaza Towers**
Opening in 1975, 28 and 42 story skyscrapers were added to the Southern Pacific Headquarters, with the resulting complex called One Market Plaza.

**Market Street**

**The Embarcadero**

**San Francisco Bay Bridge**

**Interurban Electric Railway**
A Southern Pacific subsidiary, this commuter line operated across the Bay Bridge between 1939 and 1941.

**California Street**

**Palace Hotel**

**Fremont Street**

**Vulcan Iron Works**
This locomotive builder was at Natoma and Fremont from 1861 to 1921.

**Sutter Street**

**Geary Street**

**Third Street**

**Fourth Street**

**Interstate 80 Freeway**

**80**

**Mark Hopkins House**
Unlike others of the Big Four, Hopkins never lived in his Nob Hill mansion. Instead, he lived in a cottage on Sutter near Leavenworth from which he could walk to his office at Fourth and Townsend.

**101**

**Temporary General Offices**
Between 1906 and 1917 the Offices were in temporary quarters at Powell and Market.

**Central Pacific/Southern Pacific Headquarters**
The General Offices were moved to Fourth and Townsend from Sacramento in 1873. This building, where the Big Four had their offices, was destroyed in the 1906 earthquake.

**Southern Pacific Station**
First as wooden building, later as a larger masonry Spanish-style building, the SP Depot was at Third and Townsend from 1873 until 1975 when it was moved to Fourth and Townsend. (Most of the tracks to Third were then removed.)

**China Basin**

**Townsend Street**

**Southern Pacific Yard**

**Pier 50**

**Harrison Street**

**US Highway 101 Freeway**

**Market Street**

**Southern Pacific Yard**

**Santa Fe Rail Yard**

**Harrison Street Warehouse District**

**101**

**The Mission Bay Roundhouse**
This important center of SP activities was constructed in 1909, retired in 1961 and demolished several years later.

**Potrero Hill Tunnel (Western Pacific)**

**Potrero Hill Tunnel (Southern Pacific)**

**Third Street**

# A Railroad Map of San Francisco

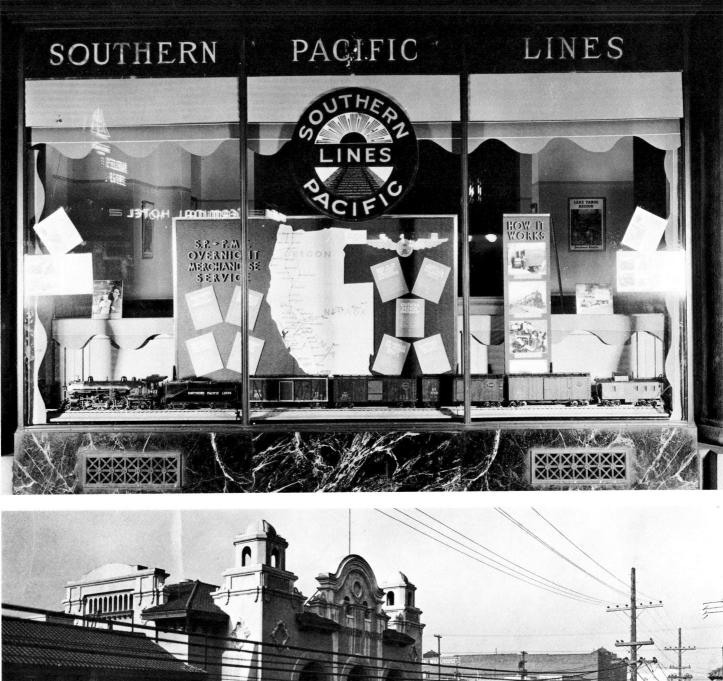

*Top:* A 1937 window display at Southern Pacific's General Office Building. Still the corporate headquarters, the building today anchors the One Market Plaza complex that includes a 42 story skyscraper built in 1975.

*Above:* The Spanish-style Southern Pacific station at Third and Townsend, shown in 1923, looking north up Third Street. Built to replace the station destroyed in the 1906 earthquake, this building was torn down in 1975.

*Above:* A Southern Pacific ticket office located at 65 Geary Street in downtown San Francisco.

*Right:* The Market Street General Office hailed the 1939 World's Fair being held at Treasure Island.

continued to live as legends long after the trains themselves have gone. They represented the glamour of an age intoxicated with the recovery from the Depression. Locomotives and cars were built with the magnificently sleek lines of high art deco, designed to give the impression of speed even while standing still. The careers of the great streamliners, interrupted by World War II, were revived in the late 1940s, only to be destroyed by the advancing technology of air and automobile travel.

Another jewel in the Southern Pacific crown was an 87 percent controlling interest in a new subsidiary, the St Louis Southwestern Railroad, or Cotton Belt, which Southern Pacific acquired in 1932 during the depths of the Depression. The Cotton Belt was an elaborate network of lines that extended from Missouri to Texas and Louisiana, where it intersected the tentacles of Southern Pacific's Sunset Route. Begun in the heart of the cotton country a half century before, the Cotton Belt had finally reached St Louis in 1903 (in time for the World's Fair), and crossed the Mississippi River into Memphis in 1912.

When the presidency of the Southern Pacific passed from Leland Stanford to C P Huntington in 1890, the center of power had passed from San Francisco to New York. With the advent of E H Harriman as president after Huntington's death in 1900, the New York headquarters became institutionalized. Operational control remained at the San Francisco general offices, which, upon completion of the 65 Market Street building, became the de facto headquarters, reducing the New York office to a kind of figurehead. In 1939 the last desk in the New York 'financial headquarters' was cleared out, and control of the nation's third largest company was consolidated in San Francisco, within clear view of the Southern Pacific ferries plying the deep blue waters of San Francisco Bay.

*Above:* The sidewheeler ferry *Sacramento* operated between the San Francisco Ferry Building and Oakland until 1958.

*Below:* This 1938 view from Southern Pacific headquarters included the recently completed San Francisco-Oakland Bay Bridge and the San Francisco Ferry Building. The spire of the 1939 World's Fair is to the left on Treasure Island.

*Above:* An interior view of the *Berkeley,* one of the last Southern Pacific ferries to ply the waters of the bay.

*Above right:* The *Klamath,* an automobile ferry, draws toward the dock to unload.

## Ferries and Bridges

The first scheduled ferry service on San Francisco Bay began in 1850. By 1930, under Southern Pacific control, the ferryboat system on the bay was the largest in the world, with 43 Southern Pacific ferries carrying 40 million passengers and 60 million automobiles annually. Within a few years of its inception, the ferryboat activity on the bay – almost entirely between San Francisco and Oakland – had become a competition largely between James Larue and Charles Minturn. In 1865 Larue sold his boats to Central Pacific, which continued to compete with Minturn between San Francisco and Oakland. In 1866 Minturn moved his operation to the north end of the bay, where he began what eventually became the ferry portion of the Northwestern Pacific, a line which in turn became a Southern Pacific subsidiary in 1929.

The Central Pacific, and later the Southern Pacific, operated the ferryboat fleets from San Francisco's Ferry Building, whose clock tower is still a major landmark at the foot of Market Street. From Market Street, the ferries crossed to the city of Alameda, adjacent to Oakland, where passengers boarded trains for points east and south. Travelers from Sacramento boarded ferryboats at Benicia for the final leg of their trip to Oakland or San Francisco. On 28 December 1879, the company began service from Benicia with the huge ferry *Solano,* a boat large enough to carry an entire train.

During the 1920s the ferries became virtual worlds unto themselves, with Christmas and New Year's Eve parties held on board. The ferry *Piedmont* even had a small putting green. Leland Stanford set the fare at 10 cents a day when the Central Pacific took over, and it stayed at that rate for decades. The ferryboat business was subsidized by other railroad activities, because the ferries were an essential link for passenger traffic into San Francisco.

In 1927 Southern Pacific put the *Fresno,* the first of three automobile ferries, into service on the bay. Three years later the Southern Pacific ferry system was at its peak, and an exemplar to the world. The Great Depression ended the upward spiral, and by the time the nation began to emerge from that Depression, another factor had been introduced to the fabric of life on San Francisco Bay.

The year 1936 was Southern Pacific's first profitable year since the onset of the Depression, but for the ferry system it was the beginning of the end. That was the year the San

Francisco-Oakland Bay Bridge opened to automobile traffic. The Bay Bridge proved to be a fast, convenient alternative to the ferry. A year later, the Golden Gate Bridge was completed, linking San Francisco with Marin County to the north. While the service to the east side of the bay continued on a smaller scale until 1958, service to Marin County ended on 28 February 1941 with the last run of the *Eureka* from Sausalito to San Francisco.

In anticipation of the Bay Bridge's construction, Southern Pacific had arranged during the 1930s to operate an electric commuter train line between San Francisco and Oakland via the bridge's lower deck. The Southern Pacific Interurban Electric Railway Company began service from a terminal at Mission and Fremont streets in San Francisco when the bridge opened in 1936. This subsidiary did not live up to the expectations of Southern Pacific, and in July 1941 the Interurban Electric was sold to the Key Route – ironically, a former rival in the ferryboat business. The Key Route rails were eventually removed from the lower deck, which was then modified for use by automobiles.

By 1951 only six of the one-time 43-ship fleet of ferryboats remained in service on San Francisco Bay. The automobile ferries *El Paso, Klamath* and *Russian River* operated between Richmond and San Rafael at the north and over the bay, while *Berkeley, Eureka* and *Sacramento* operated between the San Francisco Ferry Building and Oakland. *Stockton* and *Fresno* were sold to the Washington State ferry system as *Klickatat* and *Willapa,* while *Yosemite* sailed 9000 miles to Buenos Aires to become *Argentine,* in service between Argentina and Uruguay. The six boats still in service on the bay became four, then two; after 1958, there was none.

*Above:* **At one time Southern Pacific operated 43 ferries on the bay. Some hauled heavy loads, including full trains.**

*Above:* Southern Pacific's Interurban Electric Railway carried commuters between San Francisco and Oakland from 1936 to 1941, when it was sold off.

*Below:* The *Yosemite* was retired from service on San Francisco Bay and sold to Argentina in the 1950s.

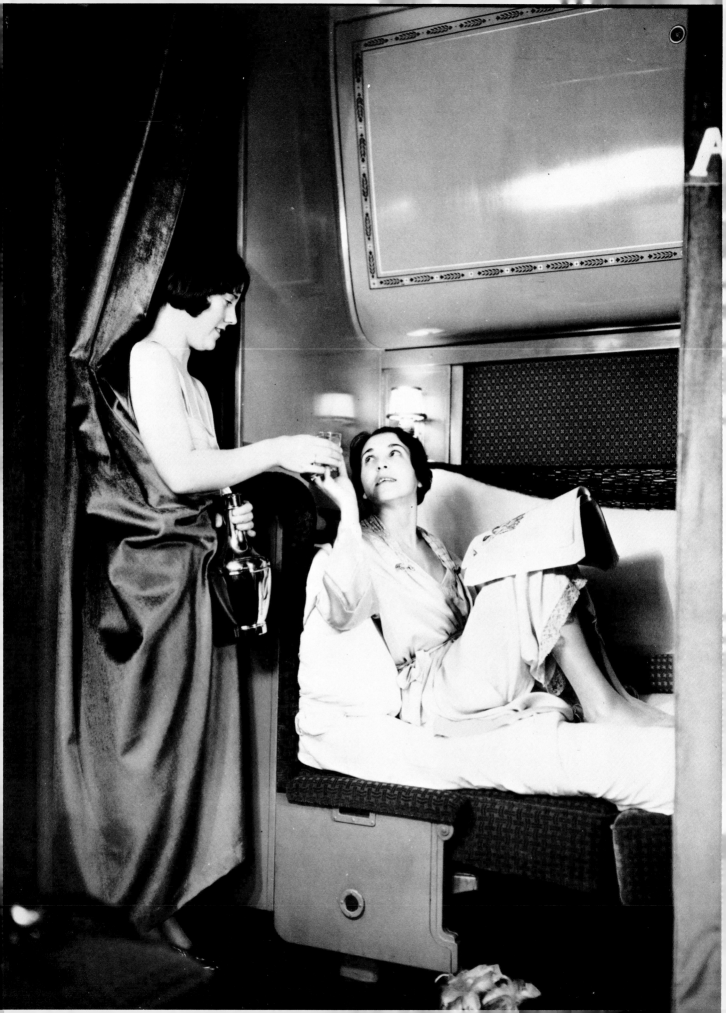

**Left: In a scene reminiscent of Maxfield Parrish, two travelers enjoy the unparalleled luxury of the famous Daylight.**

**Above, both: The Coast Daylight, No 4449, the only Daylight still in existence, has been repainted in authentic colors.**

## The Cab-Aheads

As the major railroad over most of the Far West, the Southern Pacific developed many pieces of specialized equipment to meet its unique requirements on its vast and varied rail network.

Among the most important of these were the cab-ahead (also called cab-forward or cab-in-front) locomotives. They had their genesis in two enormous 2-8-8-2 Class MC-1 (Mallet Consolidated) steam locomotives delivered to the Southern Pacific by the Baldwin Locomotive Works in 1909. These locomotives (serial numbers *4000* and *4001*) weighed 197 tons on 16 huge driving wheels, and were powered by two 26-inch high-pressure cylinders that received steam directly from a single oil-fired boiler and exhausted it directly into two 40-inch low-pressure cylinders. The engines of these articulated locomotives were designed by Samuel Vauclain at the Baldwin Works and were based on the articulated compound expansion engines developed in France by Anatole Mallet (1837-1919). The Mallet-type locomotives had been in use all over the world, and Southern Pacific's first Mallets were the first 2-8-8-2s to be built in the United States.

Engines *4000* and *4001*, articulated to handle curves better, exceeded expectations, handling 1200 tons over the Sierra at 10 mph, while using less fuel and water than earlier locomotives. The major drawback to these enormously powerful machines, however, was the tremendous heat and concentration of foul gases pulled back into the cab by the 100-foot engine. Ventilation was a problem in the miles of tunnels and snowsheds on the Sierra line, so air was pumped into the cab from the air brakes. Although the engineer could then breathe, he still had the 750-degree F exhaust temperatures to deal with. The idea that evolved was to turn the locomotive around; the cab, which was normally at the rear, would point ahead. The tender was then moved to the rear, and the cab-ahead locomotive was born. Southern Pacific was the first and only major user of cab-aheads, and they were immensely successful. One factor that made them practical for Southern Pacific as early as 1901 was that oil-powered engines were required because of the position of the tender, and Southern Pacific had been one of the first American railroads to convert its entire locomotive fleet from coal to oil.

The converted Class MC-1 locomotives were such a hit that 15 Class MC-2 locomotives were ordered as cab-aheads in late 1909. These were followed by 12 Class MC-4 freight

On the engineer's side *(top)* of the 4100 series locomotive cab, the throttle is on the upper right. The reverse lever and brake valves are to the right of the seat. The water glass and gauge cock are attached to the water column at the upper center. The view from outside the window of the fireman's side *(above)* exposes the firing valve and damping regulator at the lower left, above the steam gauge.

*Right:* In 1937 Southern Pacific purchased its first modern, more streamlined cab-heads, Class AC-7 locomotives.

*Below:* Class AC-10 cab-ahead *No 4211*, acquired in 1942.

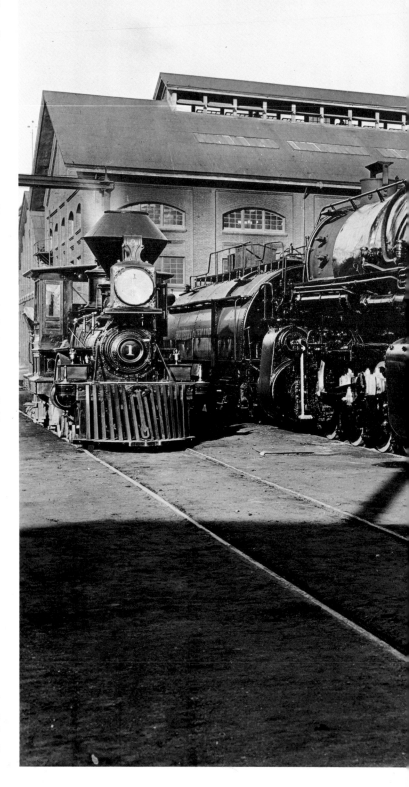

locomotives, 12 Class MC-4 passenger locomotives and 20 Class MC-6 locomotives, all ordered in 1912. These cab-aheads, or 'back-up' locomotives, were all 2-8-8-2 types except the 12-passenger locomotives, which were 2-6-6-2s, later converted to 4-6-6-2s by substituting a pair of wheels under the first box with a four-wheel truck.

In 1917 the need became apparent for a faster type of locomotive to replace the compound articulated loco-motives. Southern Pacific ordered 170 of the 2-10-2 type single expansion locomotives from the American Loco-motive Company until 1924 and an additional 4-10-2 starting in 1925. The nonarticulated locomotives resulted in rail wear, so the company's Motive Power Department studied the notion of converting the compound expansion engines of its larger existing articulated Mallets to single expansion engines. (These engines had only high-pressure cylinders in contrast to the high- *and* low-pressure cylinders of compound engines.)

The first engine to be experimentally converted at the Sacramento Shops was locomotive *No 4041*. In 1927 its low-pressure cylinders were replaced with 22-inch high-pressure cylinders and its boiler pressure was increased to 210 pounds. The net result was a locomotive half again as powerful as a 4-10-2. These locomotives, designated as Classes AC-1 through AC-3 (Articulated Consolidated) when converted, were so successful that 195 new locomotives, beginning with *No 4100*, were built in Classes AC-4 through AC-12. With redesigned boiler and upgraded systems, the new ACs represented a dramatic increase in tractive effort over the original Mallets, as indicated by the following table:

| Class and date | Tractive effort |
| --- | --- |
| Class MC-4 (1912) | 65,920 pounds |
| Class AC-1 (1927) | 90,940 pounds |
| Class AC-4 (1929) | 116,900 pounds |
| Class AC-6 (1931) | 124,300 pounds |

The Class AC-6 locomotives, beginning with *No 4126*, appeared in 1931. They were heavier than the earlier classes, but because they were articulated they generated less track wear. The last of the cab-aheads were the Class AC-12s, which weighed 658,000 pounds, more than double the weight of the Class MC-4 Mallets. The cab-aheads were originally put into service pulling heavy trains over the Sierra, but their use soon spread to the Siskiyous and eventually to the Tehachapis as well. The big locomotives became the backbone of Southern Pacific mountain operations until they were replaced by diesels in the 1950s. The last cab-ahead to make a run over the Sierra was *No 4274*, on 1 December 1956. This locomotive is preserved in the California State Railroad Museum in Sacramento.

*Above:* **Staff at the Bakersfield, California, roundhouse prepare *No 4365* for service on the San Joaquin *Daylight*.**

*Below:* **Southern Pacific trains in military service during this prewar California National Guard exercise.**

## World War II

The American entry into World War II in 1941 came at the end of Angus McDonald's $100-million investment program aimed at upgrading Southern Pacific's plant and equipment. The new switches, rails, boxcars and articulated locomotives put the railroad in a much better position to handle the challenge that was to come. The war, which had already been raging in Europe for two years, came as a surprise to few. Defense had been a national priority for over a year when the Japanese bombed Pearl Harbor. Southern Pacific had even participated, in August 1940, in the biggest mass railroad transportion exercise since World War I. Southern Pacific lines, including the Texas & New Orleans subsidiary, had co-operated with the US Army to move troops aboard 119 special military trains, meeting precise schedules. Even this massive exercise would be dwarfed by actual wartime operations. By the end of January 1942, seven weeks after the United States entered the war, 670 special military trains had been pulled over Southern Pacific lines. By the end of hostilities, the total had risen to 28,349 – enough trains to move 436 infantry divisions.

As Southern Pacific geared up to meet the needs of a nation at war, a bit of its history was swept away. When Leland Stanford drove the gold spike at Promontory, Utah, in 1869, the piece of track there was among the most important in the world. The Promontory site, meeting point of the Central Pacific and the Union Pacific, was officially Central Pacific track, because the joint terminal was a few miles east at Ogden. Promontory remained on the Central Pacific/ Southern Pacific main route until 1904, when construction of

*Above:* **Southern Pacific flatcars are loaded with M-3 Stuart tanks at the San Luis Army Ordnance Depot in 1942.**

the Lucin Cutoff rendered the Promontory route a branch line. In 1942, when the need for steel to run the nation's wartime industrial plant was desperate, the line through Promontory was eliminated and the steel rails sold for scrap. (The original gold spike had been removed in 1869.)

In deference to the historic moment at hand, a gold-plated steel spike was inserted so that it could be ceremonially pulled. Upon withdrawal of this ersatz gold spike, the rails were hauled away, and Promontory disappeared from America's railroad maps.

Unlike the World War I era, when the federal government had tried and failed to operate the nation's railroads efficiently, their management during World War II was left in the hands of the railroad companies. This policy proved prudent, since the private railroads handled 90 percent of all military matériel movements and 97 percent of troop movements within the United States. Southern Pacific alone handled 437,567 military passenger cars. Aboard these trains, some basic changes were instituted. Club cars were deleted for the duration of the war, and dining cars gave way to mass food service. The need at hand was to feed a large number of people quickly and efficiently. The cuisine was not *haute,* but it was hot, and thus much appreciated by the troops en route from boot camp to foxholes overseas.

There were changes on the lines, as well as aboard the trains. Hooded lights appeared on Southern Pacific's trains and signals, as the need for blackouts spread from the Pacific Coast to points 150 miles inland. After 19,980 Southern Pacific employees went to war, the company found itself short of many of its best operations personnel – men like Pete Matson, a dispatcher who ended up running the US Military Railroad in North Africa. Southern Pacific's female employees moved from the typing pool to the roundhouse.

The Southern Pacific, with routes extending from Portland to New Orleans, found itself with more military installations and embarkation points on its lines than any other railroad in the country. Passenger traffic on the Southern Pacific lines reached a wartime peak in 1944 that was five times the 1939 level. During that same year, the company's communications system transmitted 150,000 telegraph and 400,000 telephone messages every day!

When the war ended, Southern Pacific found itself with the more pleasant, but equally awesome, task of moving returning troops from embarkation points back to their home towns. In so doing, the railroad itself was moving from the frenzy of wartime to a somewhat smoother postwar pace that held the promise of better times for all.

## Postwar Expansion and Innovation

The years just after the end of World War II were a time of bright hopes and golden dreams for the Southern Pacific. In 1945 President Armand Mercier (1941-51) kicked off a $2-billion expansion program the likes of which hadn't been seen since the days of President Edward Henry Harriman (1901-09). New streamliners were introduced to take advantage of the surge in train travel that the company was sure would accompany postwar prosperity. Introduced in 1948, the *Golden State* reached Tucson from Chicago in 34 hours, and Los Angeles only 11 hours later. The *Daylights* that had served the San Francisco-Los Angeles Coast Route since the 1930s were augmented by the *Shasta Daylight* and *Shasta Starlight,* connecting the San Francisco Bay Area with Portland. In 1950 an all-streamlined *Cascade* overnight train was added, which made the Portland-to-San Francisco run in

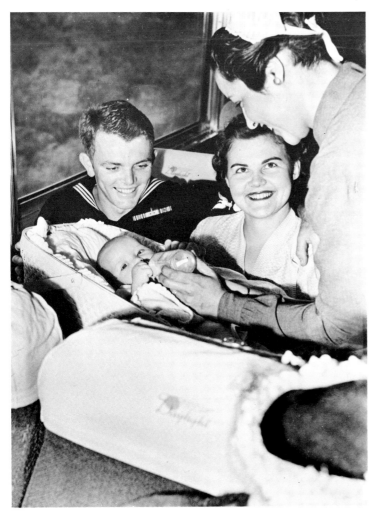

*Above:* A young family relaxes aboard the *Daylight* in 1946, back in the days before airline travel was commonplace.

*Left:* Southern Pacific Streamliner service offered excellent dining facilities and featured special children's menus.

## The Golden Century

**1938** Southern Pacific tracks are moved to make way for Shasta Dam in Northern California. The *City of San Francisco* streamliner becomes a 17-car train.

**1939** The last scheduled Southern Pacific commuter ferry run on San Francisco Bay takes place on 14 January (other Southern Pacific ferry services will continue on the bay until 1958). Southern Pacific founds Interurban Electric Railway subsidiary to run commuter trains across the San Francisco-Oakland Bay Bridge. The Southern Pacific financial headquarters in New York is closed on 13 July. The board of directors is reorganized as an all-western executive committee, the board chairmanship is abolished and those duties are merged into those of the president. The first diesel switch engines appear in the Southern Pacific fleet. Radio communications systems are installed in the Sierra.

**1940** During major national defense exercises, Southern Pacific and the Texas & New Orleans subsidiary run 119 special troop trains.

**1941** The Interurban Electric Railway subsidiary is disposed of on 26 July. Northwestern Pacific's Marin County electric trains and ferries cease operations. President Angus McDonald dies on 15 November and is succeeded by Armand Mercier. The Japanese attack Pearl Harbor on 7 December and the United States enters World War II the next day. Morgan Steamship Line service is halted as ships are needed for transporting troops (the service will not be reinstated after the war).

**1942** Southern Pacific mobilizes for war, runs extra trains and adds extra personnel as 19,980 employees join the armed services. Promontory, Utah, is removed from railroad maps as the last rails are ripped out in a wartime scrap drive.

**1944** Southern Pacific's peak year for wartime passenger traffic. The new Pecos River High Bridge is completed. Southern Pacific's last steam locomotive goes into service.

**1945** World War II ends and Congress repeals 'land grant rates,' which required railroads to carry government freight at lower rates (effective October 1946). It is estimated that by accepting these rates for government traffic, the railroads paid for land grant lands 10 times over. President Mercier launches $2 billion postwar improvement program.

**1946** Land grant rate repeal, passed in 1945, becomes effective.

**1947** Southern Pacific's first main-line freight diesel locomotives go into service. Southern Pacific (incorporated in Kentucky in 1884) is reincorporated in Delaware.

**1948** The new *Golden State* streamliner is inaugurated.

**1949** The new streamliner *Shasta Daylight* goes into service.

*Left:* The two cabs of the World War II-era 4(B-B)-class diesel-locomotive design from the Electromotive Division of General Motors placed back to back illustrate how the train could be operated in either direction without being turned. Southern Pacific ordered 20 of these 6000-horsepower locomotives in 1946 for its freight fleet. By the 1960s this design was nearly obsolete.

These diesel-electric locomotives were powered by engines that operate electric generators, which in turn furnish power for electric motors geared to the driving axles. With this type of drive, diesels could deliver almost their full horsepower the moment they started, which gave them a higher starting tractive effort than steam locomotives of comparable horsepower, somewhat more pulling power than steam locomotives at low speeds, approximately the same pulling power as comparable steam locomotives at moderate speeds, but less power than steam locomotives in fast operation.

16½ hours. Also in 1950, the new streamlined *Sunset Limited* went into service on the Sunset Route between New Orleans and Los Angeles. Described as the 'loveliest train on wheels,' the *Sunset Limited* made the trip in 42 hours, five hours less than previous trains.

Diesel locomotives became common on Southern Pacific's system by the early 1950s, though the company's lines were not fully dieselized until 1957. By the end of 1951, diesels were in use on such passenger routes as the crack *City of San Francisco*, operating over the old Central Pacific lines between Ogden and San Francisco. In January 1952 the *City of San Francisco* was trapped in the Sierra by a blizzard reminiscent of those encountered by Crocker and Strobridge when they built the original Sierra tracks nearly a century before. However, the availability of airplanes to drop supplies and of modern communications made the several days that the train spent marooned in a snowdrift more of an inconvenience than a life-threatening hardship. The episode did serve to illustrate that an end to the era of mass train travel in the United States was at hand. Although air travel had not eclipsed the steel rail as the major means of long-distance passenger transportation, it was gaining fast. The era of the grand streamliners would soon be a fading memory.

By 1954 Southern Pacific's passenger operations lost $58 million to competition with airlines and freeways. Emphasis in the company's rail operations shifted heavily toward freight.

**Southern Pacific diesels: *The City of San Francisco*, snowbound in the Sierra *(above)* and at Oakland *(right)* was jointly operated with Union Pacific and Chicago & Northwestern. In 1952, these cowgirls *(above, right)* took Southern Pacific to sunny Palm Springs.**

In 1953 Southern Pacific Motor Trucking trailers began to be 'piggy-backed' aboard flatcars to combine the volume capability of rails with the versatility and flexibility of trucks – a concept similar to the one that had resulted in creation of the PMT back in 1929. In 1955 Southern Pacific, working with the Stanford Research Institute, developed the Hydra-Cushion freight car that would provide superior protection for fragile freight. An incentive rate program was begun in 1959 to encourage heavier loading of company freight cars. New two- and three-level freight cars designed to carry automobiles were introduced in 1960 and proved extremely successful. These were supplemented with Vert-A-Pac cars, developed jointly with General Motors and introduced in 1970 between the Midwest and the Pacific Coast. Each Vert-A-Pac car could carry 30 subcompact automobiles loaded vertically. In 1971 Southern Pacific and General Motors introduced their Stac-Pac containers, which protected full-size automobiles from damage in transit.

As the company's freight operations increased, passenger operations dwindled. On 1 May 1971, the federal government's passenger rail service, Amtrak, took over operation of

*Above:* **Thirty years of intermodel freight are exemplified by the original PMT piggybacks of June 1953 *(top)* and the modern piggybacks photographed in May 1983.**

*Left:* **The Los Angeles Intermodal Depot in 1977.**

the last of Southern Pacific's intercity passenger routes, with the exception of the commuter line between San Francisco and the suburban peninsula to the south. These routes, to which the company had added 15 new double-decked passenger cars in 1968, were operated at a loss by Southern Pacific until 1980. In that year part of the financial burden was taken over by the California Department of Transportation, which considered the low-cost peninsula commuter route necessary to serve a public need.

While it was developing its engines and railcars, Southern Pacific was also busy upgrading its lines. Centralized traffic control began on the lines during World War II and spread throughout the system in the years thereafter, to be replaced by more sophisticated computerized systems as time went on.

Construction projects were another important part of postwar expansion. In 1954 the $4-million Puente Bypass was added to speed traffic around the Los Angeles terminal area.

In 1967 a $22-million cutoff or branch line was completed between Palmdale and Colton, so that trains could bypass Los Angeles altogether. This 78-mile cutoff was the longest new railroad line to be built in the United States in 25 years. Eight years earlier, the company had spent $53 million to replace the 1904 wooden-trestle segment of the Lucin Cutoff across Great Salt Lake with an earthfill causeway.

Probably the most important Southern Pacific innovation in the modernization of railroading is the Total Operations Processing System (TOPS), a real-time computer system that monitors every car, locomotive, train, engine crew, load, yard and industrial spot for a freight car on the Southern Pacific system. Entering service in 1968, TOPS quickly became a model for the US rail industry, and Southern Pacific helped install it on other major American railroads, in Canada and on the British rails.

In the way of innovation, Southern Pacific also initiated the nation's first videotype filing system to retrieve freight waybills instantly. Freight car classification yards in Houston, Texas, and Eugene, Oregon, were computerized in the late 1960s; in 1971 work began on the West Colton Yard in Southern California. When finished, the $35-million West Colton Yard was the most sophisticated in the world.

In early 1974 Southern Pacific became the first American railroad to qualify women as locomotive engineers, when Jackie Bigelow and Evelyn Newell took over the throttles of locomotives running out of Oakland. Within five years the number of women engineers at Southern Pacific had grown to over 60. In addition to jobs at the throttle, women have joined men in other traditionally male-dominated career fields. At Southern Pacific, women have become train dispatchers, electricians, machinists, brakemen and firemen. When asked about such generic titles ending in 'man,' engineer Louise Munyan replied: 'They're just names for the assignment. I know I'm a woman.'

## Diversification
The history of Southern Pacific's diversified activities outside railroading can be traced back to the nineteenth century and such entities as the Southern Pacific Land Company and the Del Monte Lodge in Monterey, where Charles Crocker died. Before the Southern Pacific was in its infancy, the Big Four had interests in a variety of enterprises. Most of these were not incorporated into the operations of the railroad or the holding company, but were personal activities. The Occidental & Oriental Steamship Company (acquired in 1872) and the

Southern Pacific's Houston Yard in 1934 (*left*) was modest compared to its 70-track Englewood Yard of 1983 (*above*). Houston is one of the busiest centers of the entire system.

*Below*: Modern freight locomotives under inspection.

*Above and below:* **Modern machinery eases maintenance, but is no substitute for the steel driving man.**

*Above:* **SPCC operated a national network of land-based microwave radio, broadband cable and satellite facilities.**

*Above:* **The Southern Pacific pipeline running under San Francisco International Airport carries jet fuel.**

*Above:* **Louise Munyan qualified as one of Southern Pacific's first woman locomotive engineers in 1976.**

Morgan Steamship Line (1883) were important, as was the elaborate ferry system that existed on San Francisco Bay for over half a century.

The Pacific Motor Trucking Company, founded in 1929, gave Southern Pacific a nascent trucking system that would parallel and enhance the rail system. In the space of 50 years, the operation grew from a pickup and delivery service in Los Angeles to three linked trucking companies covering 27,000 highway miles in 10 states, and servicing 1812 communities. In 1981 these three subsidiaries were reorganized into a single system under the Pacific Motor Transport name. Prior to the consolidation, the three subsidiaries were the original Pacific Motor Trucking Company (PMT), Southern Pacific Transport Company (SPT) and Southwestern Transportation Company (SWT), which was a subsidiary of Southern Pacific's Cotton Belt railroad subsidiary. Prior to 1981, the PMT operated in six states from Oregon to Texas, and the SPT operated in Texas and Louisiana only. The SWT's operations paralleled those of the Cotton Belt and ran north from Dallas and Shreveport to St Louis and Memphis. Today, Southern Pacific's Motor Transport Company ranks as the third biggest trucking operation in the United States in terms of intercity tonnage.

Southern Pacific is also in the pipeline business, with over 2750 miles of pipeline in Oregon, California, Nevada and Arizona and a small spur running to El Paso, Texas. In 1954

the company built its first pipelines to carry gasoline and petroleum products in Arizona, to supplement the capacity of its tank cars. Southern Pacific Pipe Lines, Incorporated (SPPL) was founded as a common-carrier subsidiary of Southern Pacific to manage the pipelines, which were extended from Los Angeles to El Paso by 1956. In Southern Pacific, SPPL joined Santa Fe Industries in the construction of the San Diego Pipeline, a 122-mile petroleum-products pipeline between Los Angeles and San Diego. Other SPPL pipelines are in operation in Oregon's Willamette Valley and under San Francisco International Airport. The SPPL pipelines are, for the most part, built on railroad right-of-way properties, simplifying construction and eliminating the possibility of environmental damage. Their operation is highly automated and constantly monitored from the SPPL headquarters in Los Angeles.

In 1970 SPPL opened the Black Mesa Pipeline, a 273-mile coal-slurry pipeline in northern Arizona. Built at a cost of $38 million, the Black Mesa Pipeline can transport 660 tons of coal slurry per hour, or 5 million tons per year. The coal is trucked from mines on Hopi and Navajo land to a slurry-preparation plant at Kayenta, Arizona. There it is reduced to powder and mixed with water to form the slurry, then pumped through the 18-inch pipeline to the furnaces of the Mohave Power Project on the Colorado River at Davis Dam, Nevada. Electricity produced at the Mohave Power Project

Houston the following year. Later in 1974 Southern Pacific became the first specialized common carrier to offer coast-to-coast service; by 1978 the new operation had turned a profit. A major advantage that SPCC had was that it paralleled the rail lines and thus could use many of the 225 existing microwave relay stations. Towers spaced 25 to 30 miles apart can transmit interference-free signals without wires. The profitable SPCC subsidiary was sold to General Telephone and Electronics (GTE) in 1982 for $740 million in cash.

The Southern Pacific Land Company, which had begun in 1870 as a means of selling off excess land grants, was reorganized in 1970 with creation of the Southern Pacific Development Company alongside the land company. The emphasis of the new subsidiary was on the development of the Southern Pacific land holdings. Within two years construction projects (ranging from shopping centers and industrial parks to hotels and resorts) were under way in 17 states. The flagship of the new series of developments was a corporate headquarters in San Francisco.

The Southern Pacific Building was opened in 1917, and it dominated the first full block of Market Street. It was gradually joined by the huge stone edifices of such other corporate giants as Pacific Gas & Electric and Standard Oil of California, which took up adjoining blocks on Market Street. By the 1960s many of San Francisco's large corporations were beginning to build steel-and-glass skyscrapers, four and five times the size of their original stone buildings. In some cases, the older buildings were knocked down to make way for the new. In other cases, like that of Southern Pacific, the older buildings were preserved. In 1973 construction began on two skyscrapers that were to link the 1917 Southern Pacific Building both visually, with same-color brick facing, and physically, by means of a huge common lobby. The new complex was completed in 1975 at a cost of $81 million. Renamed One Market Plaza, it included the old Southern Pacific Building (formerly 65 Market Street), a 28-story skyscraper, a 43-story skyscraper and extensive ground-floor retail space.

Other major development projects have included the 30-story New Orleans Hilton Hotel at the International Rivercenter and the Pacific Design Center in West Hollywood, both of which were completed in 1975. In 1981 Southern Pacific Development Company completed the Pacific Gateway Office Building on San Francisco's Mission Street, two blocks from One Market Plaza. The following year the building was sold, netting Southern Pacific $23.5 million after expenses.

Not all of the Southern Pacific Land Company's development projects are located in major urban areas. There are 450,000 acres of forest land in the Siskiyou and Trinity mountains in Northern California and in the Sierra between Sacramento and Reno. Southern Pacific's timber management program began in 1951, selectively harvesting and replanting the forests under its control. In California's Fresno County, the company's Golden Vineyards subsidiary began planting 2200 acres in eight varieties of grapes in 1972; the first crops were harvested in 1975. This is the only current instance in which the company is actually engaged in farming.

goes to the power grids of Arizona, Nevada and Southern California.

In the early days of railroad operation, Southern Pacific had to develop its own communications system to serve its far-flung outposts. The telecommunications network that began as a single strand of telegraph wire strung parallel to the first rails over the Sierra had developed into the largest private communications system in the world by 1953. By 1973 this private system had grown from telegraph and telephone wire to an elaborate line and microwave system covering 500,000 channel miles and 6800 route miles, with a 99.96 percent reliability rate 24 hours a day. The railroad's system included a complete intercity dial-telephone network serving 11,000 instruments. The system also included hundreds of channels for facsimile transmission, telemetering, train dispatching, centralized traffic control, VHF radio relay and automatic car identification. The microwave system has complete back-up capability, with emergency generators and batteries standing by at all key points.

In 1973 the Southern Pacific Communications Company (SPCC) began marketing Southern Pacific's expertise to the general public and to other corporations. The new subsidiary's operations began in 1973 between San Francisco and Los Angeles, and were extended to San Diego and

Prior to the merger with Santa Fe in 1983, the Southern Pacific Land Company was organized into three divisions. The largest is the Natural Resources Division, which manages 3.8 million acres of Southern Pacific land and an additional 1.3 million acres in California, Nevada and Utah (below which Southern Pacific controls the mineral rights). The Industrial Development Division manages 38,000 acres of well-sited industrial properties located in major market areas of 12 states. The Real Estate Division manages Southern Pacific's urban and railroad right-of-way property, totaling 30,000 acres and leased under 12,000 active leases.

Southern Pacific generally likes to put its land to productive use, which might mean building an office tower in San Francisco or grazing sheep in Nevada. In some cases, however, the holdings include land that is better left in a natural state. Such was the case with 53,000 acres in Northern California's rugged Trinity Alps, which the company offered to the federal government. These lands are now part of the Shasta-Whiskeytown-Trinity National Recreation Area.

## One Last Piece

With the exception of the Cotton Belt (acquired in 1932) and the Southern Pacific de Mexico lines (added in 1898, extended in 1927 and sold off in 1951), the overall Southern Pacific railroad map of 1980 was essentially identical to the Southern Pacific railroad map of 1890. Some sidetracks were added or deleted, including the Lucin Cutoff and the 78-mile Palmdale-Colton Cutoff, but these changes entailed by-

passes and track-straightening and did not really integrate any new territory into the system. One branch of the Sunset Route was completed in 1902 between El Paso and Tucumcari, New Mexico, but this was insignificant compared with the empire-building of the 1870s and '80s. The significance of the tracks up to Tucumcari, where they met the lines of the Chicago, Rock Island & Pacific Railroad (Rock Island Line), increased as the twentieth century progressed.

Southern Pacific's Cotton Belt had been in St Louis since 1904, where it met the Rock Island Line coming south from Chicago. The Rock Island then turned west to Kansas City and southwest to Tucumcari. In 1963 Southern Pacific expressed an interest in buying this segment of the Rock Island, because the distance between Los Angeles and St Louis would be much shorter by way of Tucumcari than by way of Southern Pacific's Texas and Louisiana lines. Agreement on the sale was not reached until 1978, after Rock Island went bankrupt. On 24 March 1980, Southern Pacific began operating on the new 992-mile line under temporary operating authority, until the $57-million deal closed in October 1980.

*Right:* In 1948 Southern Pacific took delivery of its first 6000 horsepower Alco three-unit passenger diesels. The 62-21 gear ratio gave them a top speed of 90 miles an hour on straight level track. The 197-foot-long locomotives had cabs on both ends with fixed and oscillating headlights.

*Below:* A 1954 era 2400 horsepower diesel-electric engine.

*Top:* A switch engine at work in Beaumont, Texas, at the Pennwalt Corporation plant, where agricultural chemical intermediates are manufactured.

*Above and left:* Freight is the mainstay of modern railroads.

## The Southern Pacific-Santa Fe Merger

In 1980, as Southern Pacific trains first rolled north out of Tucumcari, the company entered into serious negotiations with Santa Fe Industries regarding a merger. Negotiations continued off and on for the next three years, and on 27 September 1983 a press release was issued jointly by Southern Pacific headquarters in San Francisco and Santa Fe headquarters in Chicago stating that the two companies had agreed in principle to 'enter into a business combination.' The statement went on to say that 'Under the agreement each company would become a subsidiary of a newly formed holding company to be called Santa Fe Southern Pacific Corporation.

'The new company will combine basic transportation, natural resources, real estate and financial services, offering shareholders a broader-based enterprise and affording customers, employees and the communities we serve greater

*Left:* **In 1983 Southern Pacific Company and Santa Fe Industries announced their intentions to merge.**

*Below:* **By 1957 Southern Pacific trains were dieselized for efficiency on steep grades, curves and over long distances.**

opportunities than either company might be expected to achieve alone.

'The efficiencies inherent in this combination are necessary to maintain our competitive position in an environment wherein major railroad combinations have taken place. The strengthening of the service and financial capabilities of the combined rail operations, which will total approximately 25,000 mainline miles, will assure healthy and balanced competition in the transcontinental freight market and in regional areas.

'This combination will strengthen the existing transportation and natural resources operations of both Sante Fe Industries and Southern Pacific Company. The combination of the rail properties of the two companies will afford substantial economies and efficiencies and will result in a greatly improved capability to provide increased service to our customers. The real estate and natural resources activities of both companies complement each other and will bring geographic diversity to the new organization.'

Under the agreement, Santa Fe Industries and Southern Pacific Company are each to nominate one half of the membership of the board of directors of the new holding company, whose chief executive and operating officers will comprise officers of the two principals and their subsidiaries.

Santa Fe Industries, Incorporated, was a holding company whose major asset was the Atchison, Topeka & Santa Fe Railway (AT&SF). The AT&SF had its roots in the Atlantic & Pacific Railroad, a would-be transcontinental railroad chartered by Congress in 1866. It was designated to build west from St Louis and meet the original Southern Pacific at the California border. In 1873 the AT&SF began building southwest out of Atchison via Topeka, Kansas, along the old Santa Fe Trail. Eventually it fulfilled the plan of the now-defunct Atlantic & Pacific and reached not only the California border, but the Pacific coastline.

The AT&SF route structure covers much of the same area as the Southern Pacific. The core of the system is in Kansas and Oklahoma, with lines extended northeast to Chicago and west to Denver. Its Texas routes are mainly in the northwestern half of the state, complementing those of Southern Pacific, which are in the southeastern half. The AT&SF routes across New Mexico and Arizona cross the northern tier of the two states, paralleling Southern Pacific's Sunset Route in the south. In California AT&SF has a system that is much simpler

Santa Fe locomotives cover much the same territory as Southern Pacific's. The Tehachapi Loop *(below)* was built to help trains gain altitude to climb the Tehachapi Mountains of Southern California. The Santa Fe train pulls out of the loop and begins its ascent as the Southern Pacific locomotive emerges from the tunnel.

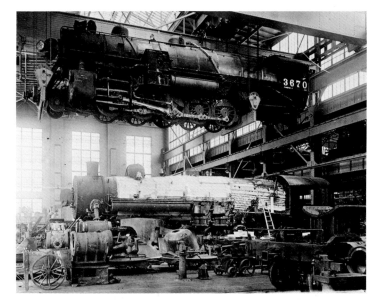

## The Golden Century

**1950** Two more new streamliners, the *Cascade* and the *Sunset Limited,* go into service. Train radios are installed on the Bakersfield-to-Los Angeles run.

**1951** Southern Pacific de Mexico is sold to the Mexican Government. The first punch-card computer system for car reporting is put into service.

**1952** The *City of San Francisco* is marooned for three days by a Sierra blizzard, but all passengers survive. The Tehachapi Line is damaged by an earthquake. A 'push-button' control system becomes operative at the Roseville Yard near Sacramento.

**1953** Southern Pacific operates its first 'piggybacks,' truck trailers aboard railroad flatcars.

**1954** Southern Pacific passenger traffic posts a loss as more freeways go into operation and potential passengers decide to drive rather than take the train. The Puente Bypass near Los Angeles is completed.

**1955** Hydra-Cushion freight cars are developed by Southern Pacific.

**1956** Southern Pacific's first petroleum pipeline goes into service between Texas and California. Electronic car classification is introduced at Houston's Englewood Yard.

**1957** Southern Pacific's locomotive fleet is now entirely diesel.

**1958** Southern Pacific ferry service on San Francisco Bay is finally discontinued.

**1959** The 1904 Lucin Cutoff across Great Salt Lake is replaced with a $53 million earthfill causeway. A rate incentive program is introduced to encourage heavier freightcar loading.

**1960** New multilevel freightcars for carrying automobiles are introduced on Southern Pacific.

**1961** The Texas & New Orleans subsidiary is merged with Southern Pacific.

**1962** Container service is introduced. Southern Pacific is the first railroad to join President Kennedy's 'Plan for Progress.' The first major Southern Pacific microwave installation is installed between Los Angeles and Fresno.

**1963** Incentive rates, introduced in 1959, along with larger freight cars have successfully expanded freight traffic.

**1964** Severe flooding causes $5 million worth of damage to Northwestern Pacific lines. Southern Pacific acquires Bankers Leasing Corporation of Boston, one of the nation's largest leasing companies.

**1965** Southern Pacific revenues from all activities top $1 billion for the first time. The ICC rejects Southern Pacific's attempt to acquire Western Pacific. The Pacific Electric Railway subsidiary in Southern California is integrated into Southern Pacific.

**1966** Southern Pacific's Black Mesa Pipeline in Arizona is begun.

**1967** Southern Pacific's Palmdale-Colton Cutoff, the longest new railroad line built in the US in a quarter century, is opened for service. The computerized classification yard is opened in Eugene, Oregon.

**1968** Computerized classification operations begin at Houston's Englewood Yard. Double-deck passenger cars are introduced on the San Francisco peninsula commuter run.

**1969** The Southern Pacific Company is reorganized into a holding company whose major asset is the Southern Pacific Transportation Company. The Southern Pacific Communications Company is formed.

**1970** The Southern Pacific Development Company is formed through a reorganization of the Southern Pacific Land Company. Vert-A-Pac rail cars for carrying 30 General Motors automobiles are put into service by Southern Pacific. The Black Mesa Pipeline begins operations.

**1972** Southern Pacific sets new records for revenues, earnings and capital improvements. The Cotton Belt is permitted by the ICC to take control of 50 percent of the Alton & Southern Railway.

**1973** Southern Pacific begins service at the West Colton rail yard in Southern California, the most modern rail yard in the world. Construction begins on One Market Plaza, a new skyscraper development adjacent to Southern Pacific headquarters.

**1974** Construction begins on the International Rivercenter in New Orleans.

**1975** The One Market Plaza skyscraper development in San Francisco and the International Rivercenter in New Orleans are completed. Southern Pacific's *No 4449* (a former *Daylight* locomotive) is selected to power the *American Freedom Train* for the US Bicentennial.

**1976** *No 4449* serves with the *American Freedom Train.* Southern Pacific handles its first unit coal train.

**1977** Revenues exceed $2 billion for the first time. Southern Pacific agrees to dispose of Pacific Fruit Express.

**1978** Southern Pacific agrees to purchase the Tucumcari-to-St

**Twentieth-century motive power on the Southern Pacific: (left to right) steam engines under repair at the Los Angeles erecting shops in 1924; an early diesel switch engine at the Owens-Illinois plant in Oakland in 1943; a postwar electric-diesel unit with cab; and a contemporary fast freight diesel.**

Louis segment of the bankrupt Chicago, Rock Island Pacific Railroad.

**1979** Southern Pacific sells 108 miles of the San Diego & Arizona Eastern Railway to San Diego for $18 million. Southern Pacific buys Ticor financial services company.

**1980** Southern Pacific's Cotton Belt begins operations on 24 March over the former Chicago, Rock Island & Pacific line that it agreed to buy in 1978 (the $57-million sale becomes final in October). Southern Pacific begins short-lived merger discussions with Santa Fe Industries. The California Department of Transportation assumes financial and marketing responsibility for the San Francisco peninsula commuter run, which Southern Pacific continues to operate.

**1981** The ICC deregulates intermodal freight operations. All of Southern Pacific's trucking operations are reorganized into the Pacific Motor Transport subsidiary. Southern Pacific introduces its Glasshopper, a covered hopper car made of fiberglass.

**1982** The Southern Pacific Communications Company (SPCC) is sold to General Telephone & Electronics (GTE) for $740 million in cash. Southern Pacific Development Company announces plans to build the Mission Bay project, a 195-acre 'city within a city' on the site of the old Mission Bay freight yard in San Francisco. An experimental geothermal power plant is built in California's Imperial Valley by Southern Pacific, Union Oil and Mono Power.

**1983** Southern Pacific Development Company revises plans for the San Francisco Mission Bay project as disruptive elements in city government block approval of the original proposal. Southern Pacific begins a program to spend $200 million over three years to install 900 miles of new main-line track. The sale of SPCC to GTE is finalized. Ticor, purchased by Southern Pacific in 1979, is sold. Northwestern Pacific sells 198 miles of track between Eureka and Outlet, California, to the New Eureka Southern Railway (effective in 1984). Santa Fe Southern Pacific Corporation is formed on 23 December, pending ICC approval, which is not expected to be immediately forthcoming.

**1984** Southern Pacific, a major corporate sponsor of the 1984 Summer Olympics in Los Angeles, operates a special passenger train from Oakland to Los Angeles on 22 July. Southern Pacific's *No 4449*, the former *Daylight* locomotive that was used to pull the Bicentennial *American Freedom Train* in 1976, is repainted in original *Daylight* colors for a special run from Portland to the New Orleans World's Fair.

**1986** The ICC will render its final decision on the Southern Pacific-Santa Fe Industries merger.

than that of Southern Pacific but serves some of the same areas: Los Angeles, San Francisco and the central San Joaquin Valley. In San Francisco the AT&SF freight yard is just across Third Street from the Southern Pacific freight yard.

The AT&SF system has 12,319 miles of track, just 15 percent less than Southern Pacific's 14,592 miles. The Santa Fe trucking subsidiary, Santa Fe Trail Transportation, serves 22 states, more than Southern Pacific's PMT, and the holding company has two pipeline systems, Gulf Central and Chaparral. Santa Fe Industries also produces and markets coal, oil and wood products.

On 23 December 1983, the Southern Pacific Company and Santa Fe Industries, Incorporated, merged to form the Santa Fe Southern Pacific Corporation, as announced on 27 September. Southern Pacific's stock was placed in a voting trust until the merger could be approved by the Interstate Commerce Commission. Under the terms of the trust, the Santa Fe Southern Pacific Corporation will be required to dispose of one of its railroads 'if the merger is not approved or if unacceptable conditions are imposed' by the ICC.

## A Portrait of Southern Pacific

Prior to the merger with Santa Fe, Southern Pacific was one of the largest railroads in the United States. Built a century ago on the dreams of four men, it grew from a tenuous steel track across hostile plains into one of the largest privately owned rail transporation companies in the world. In 1980, before the Tucumcari-Kansas City-St Louis lines added 992 miles of track, Southern Pacific owned roughly 13,600 miles of rail line connecting the mouth of the Columbia in the Pacific Northwest to the mouth of the Mississippi on the Gulf of Mexico. Its lines reach north along the Mississippi into the nation's heartland via the Cotton Belt, or St Louis Southwestern Railway, of which Southern Pacific owns 98.34 percent. But Southern Pacific is more than a railroad; it is a diversified transportation and land-development company with holdings in pipelines and telecommunications.

Southern Pacific is a vast network of steel and microwave that spans what the company calls 'The Golden Empire' and what the commentators call the 'Sun Belt.' This Golden

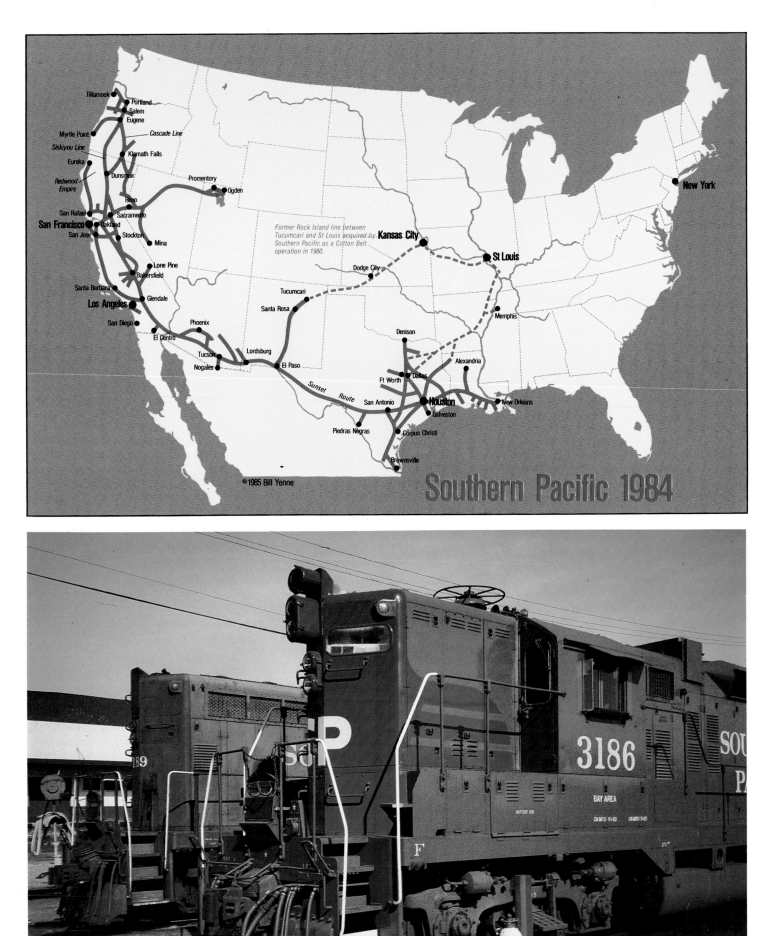

Southern Pacific 1984

Former Rock Island line between Tucumcari and St Louis acquired by Southern Pacific as a Cotton Belt operation in 1980.

© 1985 Bill Yenne

*Above: No 4449* in *Daylight* **colors crosses the Mississippi River at New Orleans for the 1984 World Exposition.**

**San Francisco *(far left)* and St Louis *(left)* are at opposite ends of the vast Southern Pacific empire.**

Empire of the Southern Pacific encompasses 12 states and touches upon three others. It is an enormous marketplace of over 70 million people – representing nearly a third of the nation's population and gross national product. The gross national product of the Golden Empire exceeds that of the rest of the nation in per-capita terms, and that of nearly every nation on earth in absolute terms. From this empire comes 97 percent of the nation's rice crop, 88 percent of its copper ore, 85 percent of its lettuce and grapes, 83 percent of its natural gas, 75 percent of its oil, 65 percent of its cotton and 40 percent of its lumber. It is a land of shimmering natural beauty and bountiful farms, the fastest-growing region in the country and the one with the most modern industrial base.

For its part, Southern Pacific is the largest and busiest transportation system in Oregon, California, Nevada, Arizona and Texas, the states that make up the heart of the Golden Empire. It serves 15 Pacific Ocean ports, 7 ports of entry into Mexico and 10 ports on the Gulf Coast.

Southern Pacific began as a golden dream to bind a continent with tracks of steel and to develop the rich resources of California and the West. In so doing, it helped bring to fruition the dreams of the millions who rode those rails to begin new lives in the West. Southern Pacific is today the legacy of the men who tamed the Sierra, saved the Imperial Valley and united California with Texas and Oregon. Southern Pacific is the men and women who built the empire of steel so that others could build their futures in the Golden Empire.

# Index

*Above:* **The men behind the Southern Pacific** *(from left to right)*: **Theodore Judah, who provided the spark that launched the dream, Collis Huntington, Leland Stanford, Charles Crocker, Mark Hopkins, Edward Harriman, Paul Shoup, Angus McDonald, Armand Mercier and Hale Holden** *(see below)*.

| President of the Central Pacific Company | |
|---|---|
| Leland Stanford | 1861-1885 |

| Presidents of the Southern Pacific Company | |
|---|---|
| Timothy Guy Phelps | 1865-1868 |
| Leland Stanford | 1868-1890 |
| Collis Porter Huntington | 1890-1900 |
| Charles Hayes | 1900-1901 |
| Edward Henry Harriman | 1901-1909 |
| Robert Lovett | 1909-1911 |
| William Sproule | 1911-1918 |
| Julius Krutschnitt | 1918-1920 |
| William Sproule | 1920-1928 |
| Paul Shoup | 1929-1932 |
| Angus Daniel McDonald | 1932-1941 |
| Armand Mercier | 1941-1951 |
| Donald Russell | 1952-1964 |
| Benjamin Biaggini | 1964-1976 |
| Denman McNear | 1976-1979 |
| Alan Furth | 1979-1982 |
| Robert Krebs | 1982-1983 |

| Chairmen of the Southern Pacific Company Executive Committee | |
|---|---|
| Leland Stanford | 1890-1893 |
| *Vacant* | 1893-1909 |
| Robert Lovett | 1909-1913 |
| Julius Krutschnitt | 1913-1925 |
| Henry de Forest | 1925-1928 |
| Hale Holden | 1929-1932 |

| Chairmen of Southern Pacific Company Board of Directors | |
|---|---|
| Henry de Forest | 1929-1932 |
| Hale Holden | 1932-1939 |
| *Position nonexistent* | 1939-1964 |
| Donald Russell | 1964-1972 |
| *Vacant* | 1972-1976 |
| Benjamin Biaggini | 1976-1983 |

*Santa Fe Southern Pacific Corporation (1983-    )*
*President:* Robert Krebs (Southern Pacific)
*Chairman:* John Schmidt (Santa Fe)
*Vice-Chairmen:* Alan Furth (Southern Pacific)
John Swartz (Santa Fe)